Kneading Jou

Kneading Journalism

Essays on baking bread and breaking down
the news

By Tony Ganzer

Edited by Brian Beesley
Illustrations by Nicole Falatic

Cherry Mountain Media
Lakewood, Ohio

Library of Congress Control Number: 2022922030
Paperback ISBN: 979-8-9873652-0-5
Hardcover ISBN: 979-8-9873652-2-9
eBook ISBN: 979-8-9873652-1-2
Audiobook ISBN: 979-8-9873652-3-6

Publisher's Cataloging-in-Publication Data

Names: Ganzer, Tony, 1984- author.
Title: Kneading journalism : essays on baking bread and breaking down the news / Tony Ganzer.
Description: Lakewood, OH : Cherry Mountain Media, 2023. | Includes bibliographical references.
Identifiers: LCCN 2022922030 (print) | ISBN 979-8-9873652-2-9 (hardcover) | ISBN 979-8-9873652-0-5 (paperback) | ISBN 979-8-9873652-1-2 (ebook) | ISBN 979-8-9873652-3-6 (audiobook)
Subjects: LCSH: Journalism. | Journalism–Social aspects. | Journalism–Study and teaching. | Mass media and public opinion–United States. | Bread. | Baking. | BISAC: LANGUAGE ARTS & DISCIPLINES / Journalism. | LANGUAGE ARTS & DISCIPLINES / Communication Studies. | BUSINESS & ECONOMICS / Industries / Media & Communications.
Classification: LCC PN4731 .G36 2023 (print) | LCC PN4731 (ebook) | DDC 070.4071/1–dc23.

Contents

The gallows and the kitchen table   1

1. Defining journalism with a bread rebellion   9

    Bake Bread: Salted French   23

2. Why journalism education can help us all   25

    Bake Bread: Rosemary   37

3. Journalists not "Journalists"   39

    Bake Bread: Irish Gingerbread   53

4. Media, Machiavelli, and Power   55

    Bake Bread: Rosemary Asiago   73

5. Bread diplomacy and Egyptian revolution   75

    Bake Bread: Egyptian Fino Bread   97

6. Get a real job   99

    Bake Bread: Whole Wheat Sandwich Bread   119

7. Leaving daily news   121

Acknowledgements   133

Bibliography   139

About the Author   159

The gallows and the kitchen table

"Rope. Tree. Journalist. Some assembly required."

Seeing these words on the back of a T-shirt might unsettle even the most hardened journalists in the best of times. When a photographer spotted one of these shirts at a campaign rally for Donald Trump in November 2016, the best of times in the relationship between journalists and members of the public had long passed, if they ever existed.

For years, it had been clear that a growing number of Americans had not-so-subtle reservations about journalists. But this shirt, to some, seemed to represent an escalation, giving a troubling look into just how broken is the relationship between some news consumers and members of the media. The shirt literally referred to a violent act against journalists, within a political and social climate that seemed equal parts combustible and unpredictable. Lynching is a horrible crime: a heinous act of brutality that wraps a violation of the human body and spirit in a cloak of perverted justice.

Here, it was reduced to a punchline on a T-shirt, making light of one of humanity's darkest acts.

Years later, on January 6, 2021, a mob filled with thousands of supporters of President Trump stormed the U.S. Capitol, with some chanting "hang Mike Pence," calling for the then-vice president to be killed. Some people went so far as to erect a makeshift gallows. This kind of nonchalance with political violence can indicate deep dysfunction of relationships, rational discourse, and respect for life.

Journalists often operate in a nexus of this dysfunction.

Depending on your viewpoint a journalist might be an agent of free speech, or a villainous slanderer, or maybe both of those extremes over the course of the same news report.

The work and identities of journalists have always been politicized and polarizing, to a degree, because all corners of society rely on the power of sharing and shaping information. A politician, celebrity, or Joe or Jane Citizen can decry the press for perceived dishonesty, unprofessionalism, or maybe just being a bad writer. It's what's supposed to happen in a free and open society, where press freedom is a fundamental right. Critique and self-reflection are baked into the system.

But rejecting a journalist's right to be alive, and right to act as a free and independent chronicler of our times, is an aberration.

Or I'd like to believe it is.

At a time when public figures can call journalists the "enemy of the people," it seems plausible that there would be shirts expressing a desire to do away with the journalists; shirts which "at the least...inflame the passions of those who either don't like, or don't understand, the news media," according to a statement from the Radio Television Digital News Association.

So how can the public better understand, if not entirely appreciate, the news media?

In an age of ever louder commentators and ever flashier technological gizmos, I would suggest starting in a place that's comfortable, non-threatening, and vital: the kitchen.

Talk of "kitchen table issues" or "kitchen table conversations" has become shorthand in our politics and journalism to describe the almost sacred ground on which neighbors and families tackle life's problems with candor and fellowship. In political campaign season, these conversations may not happen over a table, instead maybe in a diner or in someone's home.

Just about every modern politician eventually ends up trying to harness the power and familiarity of the kitchen table, even if it poses a risk. British Prime Minister Tony Blair once took an education reform plan on the road, and *The Sunday Times* noted, "the kitchen table conversation over tea and chocolate biscuits left some of the parents less than impressed," with one considering sending her kids to private school instead, and demanding her tax money back.

The kitchen table is for modern-day hunting, gathering, and relating to one another.

The power of the kitchen table is easily recognized, but not easily harnessed.

Traditionally the table acted as a place to sit, lay out papers, and look each other in the eyes while trying to figure out the whats, whys, and hows of the everyday. It's a place to strengthen family bonds, share stories, and reinforce structure for children. The American College of Pediatricians described the family table as "one of the very few places that children can observe their parents interact, negotiate, solve problems, express emotions and treat one another with respect."

Yes, **treat one another with respect.**

I'm more used to *kitchen conversations*, minus the table. The kitchen talk usually involves making a meal, or in my case baking a loaf of bread. Just as we come together to feed our minds and souls in conversation, we're preparing sustenance for our bodies — a modern-day hunting-and-gathering-and-relating to one another.

In turbulent political times conversations can gravitate toward hot-button or delicate issues, and depending on the circumstances those conversations can cut deep. So divisive is the topic of politics that *Psychology Today* offered a short list of tips to survive the endeavor during the holidays, beginning with a call to "remember that other peoples' opinions are not a referendum on your opinions." That tip is only worth mentioning because our society is forgetting (has forgotten?) how to share, and grow, and explore issues without seeing the conversation as an attack on who we are, or who we wish to be.

Journalism is supposed to help the public have these conversations in intelligent ways. Pioneering journalist Edward R. Murrow said famously that television can teach, enlighten, and inspire, if it's used to do so. That statement can easily extend more broadly to journalism in every medium.

But that T-shirt referencing lynching shows us there's a serious problem.

The covenant between the public and journalists has, for quite some time, been strained, damaged, or broken into a million skepticism-filled pieces. Trust and what is considered trustworthy seem to be fickle things in media generally, but audiences have continued to seek refuge in ever more solidified ideological echo chambers.

Critics complain about a monolith dubbed *the media* without thinking about what that *really* means. *Media* is a term devoid of nuance. The term is broad, coarse, and does us no favors in pinpointing what we're actually talking about: Does *media* mean journalism as a craft? Does *media* mean legions of anonymous online commenters fueling outrage? Does *media* mean any of a variety of news-gathering or news-disseminating outlets, from newspapers and broadcasters, to podcasters, bloggers, or pamphleteers?

As with any word, the context in which it's used is incredibly important, and *media* has become something else: a bogeyman seeming to represent everything and nothing, all at the same time.

Media doesn't seem to be used very often to mean flesh-and-blood people; the individual television hosts, pundits, or journalists living as your neighbors, relatives, or fellow citizens who happen to join you to bake some bread, eat some chocolate biscuits, and have potentially stimulating and enlightening conversations.

Dealing only with a bogeyman is a victory for people who embrace over-simplification. By avoiding the details one can complain about *the media's* sensationalized reporting, with culpability shared by any journalist, without distinction. This blurring of practice and practitioner is dangerous and counter-productive.

It dehumanizes journalists.

Journalism was my profession, but also my vocation. The skills, mindset, and training I received as a journalist inform all aspects of my life, and make me a more discerning and curious citizen.

And yes, this vocation also seasons my amateur bread baking, and the two have long been linked. After graduating with a bachelor's degree in journalism, I worked as an assistant baker in a food cooperative. I'd spend a few early mornings a week shaping baguettes and stocking loaves of wheat bread, in between short stints as a contract reporter for a regional public media network serving stations in Idaho, Oregon, and Washington State.

Bread remained a minor but present character during my time as a morning producer and radio reporter in Phoenix; as a guest editor at public media outlets while on a fellowship to Germany for young American professionals; as a national radio correspondent in Switzerland; and as a drive-time radio host and reporter in Cleveland. Even before the global COVID-19 pandemic kindled in many an interest in home baking, I had begun baking all sandwich and artisan breads for my family as an exercise in knowing exactly what ingredients were in our bread, while also feeling a sense of empowerment through hand-making a fundamental part of the family diet.

The combination of baking and thoughts on the craft of journalism may seem to be a silly mash-up, but it's driven by serious impulses. Just as the kitchen table is a place for friends and families to talk about politics, finances, or health issues, this sacred ground can frame a conversation about journalism.

Kneading Journalism extends both an olive branch, and maybe a slice of olive bread, to fellow critical thinkers who are interested in bite-sized thoughts on journalism and society. But ideas about what journalism is, what it could be, and what it mustn't be, are as complicated as they are diverse.

This book is made up of essays on journalism topics that are, in many cases, inspired by and built out of shorter essays from my website. I also provide recipes for the loaves of bread I bake, just as clear as I hope my essays are. If you choose to bake a bread along with me, you should be able to read and digest the accompanying chapter while waiting for the bread to rise.

If we want to take a critical and nuanced view of journalism and how we want to be informed, and break bread together, we should first bake the bread.

1. Defining journalism with a bread rebellion

It seemed a recipe for disaster. A neighborhood woman in the Paris suburb of Saint-Antoine looked to buy a 4-pound loaf of *bis-blanc*, an average mixed bread of white and wheat flour, for a price of 12 sous. The price she offered wasn't unreasonable by market standards, but the baker manning the store wasn't interested in haggling. He priced the loaf at either 13 or 14 sous (depending on who you ask) and wouldn't budge.

"Since you won't give me a bread for my money, I'll have it for nothing," the woman yelled, as she snatched the loaf and made for the door.

Tensions between French bread buyers and bakers had reached a fever pitch by July 1725. A poor grain harvest strangled supply across the country, including in Saint-Antoine. Soaring bread prices, hunger, and frustration over the situation would erupt in violence that could be considered a foretaste of the revolution to come more than six decades later.

The woman's attempted theft — she gave the bread back after a confrontation — ended in her throwing rocks at the bakery, supported by an increasingly agitated crowd, which the authorities had to break up. But this wasn't an isolated incident. It might be seen as foreshadowing another loaf theft and full-scale riot just weeks later; an act of rebellion and protest against the ruling class, and against powerful bakery owners like Louise Chaudron, a widow.

Chaudron's operation used twice as much wheat as the average baker, and provided about double the average amount of bread to the markets. In an attempt to maximize profits, Chaudron apparently conspired with other bakers to raise bread prices out of proportion with grain prices. That was at least an accusation against her, as hungry and frustrated crowds rallied around the bread thief.

Chaudron's affluence, and reputation as a "rogue" baker among some commoners, attracted the protests to her shop. The tensions may have been fueled by the results of a police raid on Chaudron's bread market stall a month before, when investigators discovered unmarked and underweight loaves.

"Since you won't give me a bread for my money, I'll have it for nothing."

Even more than it does now, bread in the 18th century fueled French society before, through, and after its revolution. Bread today is still a staple of French society and identity to a degree, but in the time of the *Ancien Régime* (Old Regime) access to bread equated very much to access to life, especially for the underclass ruled by Louis XV.

We know about Chaudron, and the theft of a loaf of *bis-blanc* because of a collection of documentation including police reports, and witness statements from the time, filed in national archives, brought to life by history (and bread) scholars like Cornell's Steven Laurence Kaplan, who pieced together the drama of Saint-Antoine. Journalism, as we know it today, didn't really exist yet — elements of contemporary journalism, yes, but not the craft as you might think of it. The police and royal guards can tell us that many in the mob were beggars, or that they took 600 to 900 pounds of bread from Chaudron alone. Select details of the situation might have appeared in almanacs, newsletters, or personal journals.

But this information isn't contained in a form necessarily meant for the masses, and not meant to help empower the masses with knowledge.

There wasn't a true freedom of expression or freedom of the press under the Old Regime. Writing in papers or pamphlets tended to be literary in nature, or of science and the arts. Political writing — and discontent — stayed mostly underground. A new kind of journalism, as something closer to what we might recognize, would soon appear on the horizon, in many forms.

Journalism contains multitudes

Sometimes the simplest questions are the most difficult to answer, and "What is journalism?" is no exception. It seems that most people have an idea of what the characteristics of journalism are, and what they think it should look like or sound like, but a simple and clear definition can be tough. Definitions and attitudes about what is acceptable or not can shift depending on your viewpoint.

A natural place to look for a formal definition is the dictionary. Merriam-Webster's defines journalism as:

1.

  (a): the collection and editing of news for presentation through the media

  (b): the public press

  (c): an academic study concerned with the collection and editing of news or the management of a news medium

2.

  (a): writing designed for publication in a newspaper or magazine

  (b): writing characterized by a direct presentation of facts or description of events without an attempt at interpretation

(c): writing designed to appeal to current popular taste or public interest

This definition is a good effort, but might be troublesome.

Take for instance the first definition: the collection and editing of news for presentation through media. But what media? Does that matter? Is a blogger always committing an act of journalism if he or she collects news of *any* kind? (We'll talk more about who is a journalist, including bloggers, and who is committing acts of journalism in Chapter 3.)

Definition 2(b) is also on shaky ground. If journalism is presenting facts without an attempt at interpretation then where does news analysis fall on the spectrum of a journalist's skill set? Or in an investigative report, at the point where a journalist explains what the trail of facts shows, or a data set illuminates, is that not journalism because it interprets what has been learned?

Maybe this is intentional nitpicking at the language around journalism after a noble attempt by a dictionary, but I do it only to show that the issue can get murky when trying to reach the essence of *journalism*.

The American Press Institute defines it as an activity, and what comes from the activity. Journalism is "the activity of gathering, assessing, creating, and presenting news and information. It is also the product of these activities." And the value of that journalism "flows from its purpose to provide people with verified information they can use to make better decisions, and its practices, the most important of which is a systematic process...that journalists use to find not just the facts, but also the "truth about the facts."

This is a solid definition of journalism. But we need to keep in mind how messy the world is, and that mess is represented by many perspectives on how to do journalism, and how to rate the quality of the final product. Alan Rusbridger, a former editor-in-chief of *The Guardian* newspaper in the U.K. summed up the problem in an interview:

> "We talk about journalism, and journalism is Fox News and journalism is The New York Times and journalism is the Daily Mail and the BBC. All of those places have completely different ideas of what journalism should be and that's confusing for the public. And then you have journalists who are themselves confused about what our role is."

There are many interpretations and implementations of the craft of journalism, some of them resulting in something more akin to public relations for a cause, than something held to certain norms in service of the public. Sensationalized news stories with exaggerated details that made up the yellow press or yellow journalism were still a kind of journalism. The term "yellow journalism" originated during a fierce battle over readers between 19th century New York newspaper publishers William Randolph Hearst and Joseph Pulitzer. Hearst had hired away a cartoonist from Pulitzer, whose comic *The Yellow*

Kid was printed in color. As the publishers escalated their efforts to push up profits and capture readers from each other, their papers' reporting methods and presentation of world events became increasingly sensationalized, culminating in the fanning of anti-Spanish sentiment ahead of the Spanish-American War.

Hearst and Pulitzer's profit-driven roles around that war lacked in research or verified facts, and emphasized the shock factor to earn sales. It was journalism, but perhaps bad journalism, or flawed, incomplete, discriminatory, negligent journalism — at least by modern standards.

Journalistic malpractice is not limited to the distant past. During the U.S. invasion of Iraq in 2003, many journalists did not press the administration of George W. Bush for full documentation of claims about alleged weapons of mass destruction held by the dictator Saddam Hussein, and more aggressively question the justification for war. Howard Kurtz, a journalist who covers the media, called it "the media's greatest failure in modern times [...] All too often, skepticism was checked at the door, and the shaky claims of top officials and unnamed sources were trumpeted as fact." You might call it a sin of omission by news outlets failing to complete journalistic due-diligence amid political drum beats for war. News reports from that time still qualify as journalism, albeit deeply flawed journalism which erodes public trust, and as Kurtz wrote, "casts a dark shadow on the news business that has not entirely lifted."

Decades after the bread riots of Saint-Antoine a new kind of press emerged with the energy of the Enlightenment, but bread was still an important catalyst. By one analysis, more than 140 new publications sprang up by the end of 1789, reflecting the voices of a nation publicly and violently transforming itself. Regardless of the governing structure, citizens and communities worried that grain shortages or mismanaged price and supply regulations would lead to further panic. It can be seen as a kind of progress that one official was the subject of a grain-related political pamphlet accusing him of "A Plot to Famish Paris" in 1793, leading to an investigation of sorts and exoneration, instead of that official being targeted by a violent mob from the outset.

France in the 18th century is obviously a very different media ecosystem than we have today. But it's not entirely foreign. It was a dynamic environment, with Enlightenment entrepreneurs creating pamphlets and publications that fulfill particular political purposes, niches, or viewpoints, with titles like the *Patriote françois*, *L'Ami du peuple*, or the royalist *Actes des Apôtres*. This mediascape is rebellious and opinionated.

Tensions between French bread buyers and bakers had reached a fever pitch by July 1725.

News columns and editorials in modern times are considered part of journalism, and they're even honored by Pulitzer Prizes, this despite the fact that a clear opinion is given and an argument is made in the work. It's a different kind of journalism than daily news reporting, to be sure, but the methods used to craft the piece are journalistic. Many editorial writers invest greatly in researching, sourcing, and fact-checking their pieces so as to best make their point, while also standing up to the inevitable public scrutiny of their work. Of course, there are also editorial writers who do little of this.

Television talk shows or websites that blatantly paint stories in a way meant to help or harm a political cause or party are still a kind of a journalism, and the partisanship shown by them is not new. It was seen in many revolutionary French publications, but also in the early years of the United States. Then, journalism encompassed partisan papers like the Democratic-Republican *National Gazette*, backed by Thomas Jefferson and James Madison, or the Federalist *Gazette of the United States*, backed by Alexander Hamilton. A partisan paper can still employ journalistic methods, albeit for its own political purpose.

Final thoughts

The core of what journalism should be, in my view, is a craft of true-life storytelling which holds to a standard of ethics and uses a particular set of methods and skills in service to the public good — have an eye on government, figure things out, explain and identify trends, introduce a character, place, or event that illustrates life in a particular area, etc. The common thread is that the work is always in service to the news consumer and the community. Among a journalist's particular skills would be the ability to listen, research, write, interview, contextualize and analyze information.

Traditional journalists endure the best and worst society can produce. Those in the news business are paid to read, interpret, investigate, and experience tragedy and triumph within calibrated limits. The latest realities of war must be relayed in just minutes of airtime. A complicated piece of legislation must be decoded and explained in column inches, not pages. A scientific break-through must be distilled into a 90-second TV package, or maybe less. Even with the infinite space of the web, there is still a time pressure: get the story posted quickly, lest you be scooped.

I was taught — and am still mentored — by journalists who champion a kind of fundamentals-heavy approach to the news business. Stories are meant to be told clearly, accurately, and concisely. Do research. Account for cultural nuance. Consider your own bias. Confirm information: sometimes people manipulate the truth or out-right lie.

These are not really secrets to journalism, but rather signals of a back-to-basics approach to our contemporary understanding of how journalism has evolved. It's about appreciating the craft, and trying to safeguard the profession from ourselves, our biases, our history, and our error-prone humanity. Years ago I found refuge in an early edition of The *Elements of Journalism* by Tom Rosenstiel and Bill Kovach. The book is a tremendous deep dive into the duties, characteristics, and tension that exists in modern journalism, exploring everything from perceived bias, to news values, to newsroom culture. The book makes a case that journalistic method is meant to be objective, not necessarily the journalist with their own set of experiences, perspectives, and biases. Journalism then becomes like a science, following a scientific method for independent truth-finding in service of the public. Fairness is subjective and incomplete if used as the sole guiding factor in journalism, because simply airing many sides of an issue doesn't necessarily provide context to the issue at hand. Fairness alone can actually tilt discussion of a topic away from reality, detracting from the integrity of reporting just as any other fault would, such as journalists interviewing sources who are friends, promoting stories in which the journalist has a history or personal affiliation, or journalists themselves becoming a character in the story. Modern journalists are ideally expected to be independent, honest, and transparent in their service to the public interest, as opposed to their own, with this "scientific method" helping to inoculate reporting from malicious and accidental forces.

"The quality of the news about modern society is an index of its social organization," author, journalist, and commentator Walter Lippmann wrote in 1922. "The better the institutions, the more all interests concerned are formally represented, the more issues are disentangled, the more objective criteria are introduced, the more perfectly an affair can be presented as news. At its best the press is a servant and guardian of institutions; at its worst it is a means by which a few exploit social disorganization to their own ends."

My career in journalism was for me more akin to a vocation or calling than a profession, with the "scientific method" of journalism influencing who I was in and out of the newsroom. I naturally tried to think about issues in non-partisan terms, in order to try to parse politics from reality. I thought about and categorized information in a way that considers how it might factor into a story down the road from which the general public might benefit. I asked questions with curiosity and tenacity, but also with empathy. I guarded my personal opinions so as not to lose my standing as a curious advocate for the general public, in its many forms.

This vocation exists independent of my actual job title. If I choose to bake *bis-blanc* in my own *boulangerie* (bakery), the way I read, research, and interpret information will still be influenced by this vocation. Not every journalist is like this, but some are.

The world is a messy place, filled with fragmented ideas of what society should look like. That fragmentation is reflected also in our journalism: it's in the straight news stories by the marquee publications, and it's in the blatantly partisan outlets committed to particular causes or ideologies. Our task is to be aware of what kind of journalism we're interacting with, and whether we're okay with it. If we're not, we should demand better from our reporters, editors, publishers, and executives.

Defining journalism is not easy. But hopefully with these few thoughts, we can start to wrestle with the questions of which elements of journalism we want to support, and how we can restore the public's trust in the compact between journalists and the people they're supposed to serve.

Bake Bread: Salted French

This is a bread for all occasions, and one that's fairly simple to make. It's fine to snack on, and pair with some cheese or jam, or with a larger meal.

You need:

Active dry yeast: 4 tsp
Sugar: 3 tsp
Warm water: 3 cups
Flour: 6 cups (unbleached is better, bread flour is best, but use what you have!)
Salt: 2.5 tsp
Cornmeal (optional): 1 Tbsp

1) Mix yeast, sugar, and warm water in a bowl. Let sit for a couple minutes until the yeast begins to foam. Stir lightly.

2) Mix in flour and salt until the dough isn't so sticky and starts to firm up. If you're using a stand mixer keep it on low to medium speed.

3) Once your dough is in a workable form, transfer it to a lightly floured workspace. Begin to knead the dough, turning it and shaping it, while bringing in flour as necessary. You don't want the dough too sticky, or too dry. The more you bake, the easier it gets to have a feel for it!

4) Place the dough into a greased/oiled bowl, and let rest 60 mins or until doubled.

5) Punch down the dough on your lightly floured workspace, and divide into two. Shape the loaf into a round. Lightly dust a banneton with rice flour (or similar) for the loaves to rise for another 45 minutes or so. Alternatively, set the loaf/loaves on a greased/oiled pan to rise. You can also form baguettes (250 grams each) or bread rolls at 65-90 grams each. This dough works in many forms! Preheat oven at 470F.

6) Transfer your loaves onto a baking pan if they aren't already on it. You can sprinkle cornmeal on the pan if you want, and set the dough on it. With a sharp bread knife or lame, cut one line into the top of the loaf.

7) Spritz the loaves with water, or you could use a light brushing of oil. Sprinkle salt on top.

8) Bake 20-25 minutes until brown and tapping the loaves produces a hollow sound. If you opted for rolls be sure to check them before the 20 minute mark.

9) Let cool, and dig in!

2. Why journalism education can help us all

A morning huddle of commuters through the Munich train station brought little distraction from the sting of February cold, especially for residents surviving on the streets. The normal route to my temporary job placement with a German public radio station brought me past one such survivor regularly. His clothes were covered with the product of months, maybe years, of street life. He usually had a shopping cart with four or five suitcases on it, positioned near a retail bakery on the edge of the station's boundary.

On this morning the man didn't have a cart, and he sat rocking against the base of a concrete box, his hands between his thighs for warmth. Even retail chain bakeries in Germany offer scores of baked goods for relatively low prices, be it *Dinkelbrot* (spelt bread), or a *Käsebrötchen* (cheese bread roll), or a croissant. I bought an extra large croissant, and put it in its own bag before approaching the man.

"Möchten Sie ein Croissant?"
"Would you like a croissant?" I asked, his head snapping up from the hypnotic cold.

"Ja, bitte. Das wäre sehr nett von Ihnen."
"Yes, please, that would be very nice of you," he said appreciatively with a strained, yet strong voice.

"Danke, sehr. Danke. Schönen Tag noch."
"Thank you, very much," he said as I gave him the croissant, and said goodbye.**"Thank you. Have a great rest of your day."**

A man cannot live by a croissant alone, and this is not a substitute for any substantive social aid or support a person might need. But maybe for a man who needed a bite to eat, and perhaps a friendly face to acknowledge his existence, this interaction could be seen as positive.

Bakeries are everywhere in Germany, from kiosks offering basic pretzels or rolls, to cheap retail shops offering mass-produced fare, to more traditional family-run operations.

Bread is baked into the German economy, with Germany being the European Union's second-largest wheat producer behind France (supplying bakers and brewers alike.) Germans bake so much bread that it actually goes to waste at an alarming rate, with one study estimating 1.7 million tons of German baked goods recorded as losses per year. In some medium-sized operations, the conservancy organization WWF estimated every fifth product was wasted.

A journalist's day exists at the intersection of research, general reading, interviews, conversations, and events, leading oftentimes to threads of information to be stored away in a notebook or memory. Journalists tend to develop certain skills to help weave the threads into clearer pictures of society at a given moment in time.

On one level, you might hear an anecdote about giving a man something to eat outside a bakery and think of it as an isolated interaction with no connection to a bigger picture. But the journalist's perspective puts that interaction in a larger context: perhaps in terms of the greater homeless population; perhaps of how tax money is or is not supporting social services; or perhaps in the context of an over-productive and possibly wasteful bakery industry.

One interaction then becomes a window to a bigger story.

A man cannot live by a croissant alone.

The same skills which might help a journalist contextualize smaller moments in society can benefit anyone wanting to be an even more engaged citizen, consumer of news, and student of our world today.

Teaching Journalism

Students are, sometimes jokingly, warned away from an undergraduate education in journalism or media studies because the craft of journalism is one honed, or not, through a career. The basics could be picked up on the job, an argument goes. No journalism degree is necessary, and in fact other specialties — politics, economics, history, etc. — would be cherished more.

The Poynter Institute, a nonprofit that provides journalism training and support, once aggregated four arguments against a journalism degree. These included the need for new technological skills which are learned elsewhere, or the importance of on-the-job trial-and-error for advancement, more than a degree. And it's true: the profession *is* changing, and technology *is* evolving at a pace faster than many media outlets can handle effectively.

But these arguments about what journalism education is or should be, are as old as modern journalism education itself.

Legendary newspaper publisher Joseph Pulitzer founded one of the earliest American journalism schools, the Columbia School of Journalism, after a long fight to justify the necessity of formal education. In an essay in 1904, Pulitzer countered the argument that journalism can be simply taught on the job. "What is the actual practice (purpose) of the office?" Pulitzer wrote. "It is not apprenticeship. It is work, in which every participant is supposed to know his business. Nobody in a newspaper office has the time or the inclination to teach a raw reporter the things he ought to know before taking up even the humblest work of the journalist."

Pulitzer's defense of formal journalism education is multifaceted and familiar. He saw journalism as vital to a community, with the work being in the public interest, and not just in interest of profits. To serve that lofty mission, Pulitzer thought courses should be varied and sweeping: in communication and writing, in law, in ethics, literature, history, sociology, economics, statistics, modern languages, science, and more. The bulwark of democracy, it seems, would be a public informed and advocated for by well-educated, adaptable, hyper-generalists.

Decades later, mass communications scholar Wilbur Schramm wrote about journalism education as one needing to be "aimed at perspective, understanding, and broad competence." In all of society, Schramm wrote, who has more need than a professional communicator "for the qualities which general education is intended to evoke?"

Schramm cites efforts in professionalizing journalism education funded with help from the Carnegie Foundation for the Advancement of Teaching. In modern times, Carnegie Corporation of New York and the John S. and James L. Knight Foundation launched an initiative to explore education for the future of journalism. Here, too, diversity was important, with multidisciplinary studies being keys to helping young journalists be adaptable to a world in flux.

But remember to focus

Bread is serious business in Germany.

The country has nearly 3,200 officially recognized types of bread, according to the *Deutsches Brotinstitut*, the German Bread Institute. On the institute's website, you can search for a proper bakery nearby or download the Baker Finder app, you can learn about bread sommeliers (kind of like wine sommeliers who are specialists in all things wine, but with bread instead), or find an online course to learn about, yes, all things bread.

With such investment in the bread industry, maybe it's no surprise that so much bread is wasted. Shoppers are less likely to go into a bakery with empty shelves, so the well-trained bakers load them up every day, hoping to entice an increasingly carb-conscious public. Bakers seem to have specialized in so many kinds of products, delicious though they may be, that the industry's business strategy relies on a wide net: appeal to nearly all bread consumers, with many options, and with full shelves.

While multiple specialties may contribute to waste in the bread industry, for journalism it might be the only option. The craft of analyzing, contextualizing, understanding, distilling, and relaying information is much easier when drawing upon a broad background.

Multiple specialties may contribute to waste in the bread industry, for journalism it might be the only option.

Journalism, as with the bread industry, has also long faced economic pressures. Schramm pointed out in 1947 that journalism schools naturally taught radio skills, advertising, or typography, because the market demanded them, and what good were graduates who couldn't fulfill what the market demanded?

Modern schools, too, are adjusting to try to anticipate how students will best find work and perhaps fulfill that altruistic service role of journalism. This can be seen in the rise of programs catering to multimedia journalists (MMJs) trained to be one-person field correspondents and videographers, or programs teaching data-driven reporting and computer skills. The modern Carnegie/Knight initiative also pointed to efforts at multidisciplinary programs giving students a head-start in a given area of focus, or beat, in subjects like public health or economics.

Multidisciplinary programs à la carte can be pricey, though. If a student goes to Pulitzer's Columbia Journalism School for a master's degree in data journalism, the school's website estimates the total cost (albeit including all tuition, fees, and estimated living expenses) at $152,372 — nearly two-and-a-half times the annual 2018 mean wage for a radio or television correspondent ($64,820). And that wage is affected by geography and market-size, meaning smaller markets can face much lower wages, increasing the time and effort it may take to work off school debt. Undergraduate degrees cost less, of course, but unless the economy would raise the wages for and perceived value of a journalist, it's a difficult financial case to make.

With the exception of some specialized skills, many of the subjects valued by multidisciplinary journalism programs are really just keys to a strong general education. Pulitzer's argument, in a sense, was for the education and professionalization of good thinkers, researchers, and citizens. A flair for storytelling and writing might set the journalist further apart, but Pulitzer's goal remains relevant.

Final thoughts

There are at least two important questions to think about when it comes to journalism education: how are we educating journalists, and how can the characteristics of journalism help the general public?

For journalists, I would welcome Pulitzer's all-of-the-above strategy, but there are also necessary basics:

- News judgment (Answer who, what, why, when, where, and how. Know what qualifies as a relevant news item about money, crime, politics, education, public figures, more)
- Know how to construct a news story, and write clear and concise copy
- Know how to think critically about subjects or types of media manipulation
- Know how to research with and without a computer
- Know how to interview
- Know how to translate news stories into plain language

Formal journalism education in a university setting also offers other benefits, such as providing an incubator for journalists not fully formed. They can give a taste of doing the real thing, through internships, school papers or radio/TV stations, and practical coursework, which all give a budding journalist time to, you know, practice. Those early years are supposed to be a time during which a student can screw up and not be relegated to another profession out of disgrace.

I was fortunate to gain a lot of experience in the early days of my journalism life, providing hard lessons with a soft landing. It was in college I was given the straight opinion of a newspaper city editor who bled red ink onto my stories until I produced something passable. It was where I first experienced a CD malfunction while hosting a radio program, and heard the deafening silence of dead air.

College was also where I first interviewed local politicians, and had a certain buffer zone between my inexperience and their swagger. As a student radio reporter I opted to host election night coverage that paid special attention to the local issues of my university town in Idaho. I recall interviewing one candidate for state senate who was a known quantity in local politics, with a long history of activism. I posed to him my prepared questions, and listened intently as he made claims and proposals in elevated prose. In hindsight, I didn't know enough about the issues or this candidate to conduct as effective an interview as I would now hope. I sat listening, and nodding, but I wasn't prepared to act as a curious proxy for the public. Later in my career, whether interviewing the president of Switzerland about renewable energy or the governor of Ohio about why he was in Davos, I put in more effort to know the person and the issues being discussed, and hopefully create a more fulfilling interview for the public.

There is always a little training when starting a new job, but some things should have been taught and mastered before a staffer enters a newsroom, as Pulitzer said. It is true many of these things can be picked up on the job, but what harm is there to expect (or desire, at least?) the bar to begin a little higher than ground-level? Even a four-year degree of mini-failures can mature a young journalist enough to be that much more ready for prime-time in a newsroom.

In an age of punditry, 24-hour news cycles, and an over-load of fiction passing as vital information, there would seem to be no benefit in having fewer folks trained in news judgment, ethics, and the sense of civic responsibility which make for a quality Fourth Estate. As is increasingly apparent, in the U.S. and elsewhere, when the quality of media suffers, democracy also suffers, because the public square becomes intellectually impaired; outnumbered by appeals to emotion.

It is okay to demand more from journalism. And society would be stronger if we all valued more of the basic skills needed to fulfill the profession's noble task.

Bake Bread: Rosemary

A bread to be an appetizer, or perhaps to pair with a pasta dish. Eat plain, with butter, or even seasoned olive oil.

You need:

Warm water: 1 cup
Sugar: 1 Tbsp
Active dry yeast: 2.5 tsp
Salt: 1 tsp
Olive oil: 1 Tbsp
Rosemary: 2 Tbsp
Unbleached white flour: 3 cups
Butter: 2 Tbsp

1) Mix sugar, yeast, and warm water in a bowl. Begin to stir, waiting for bubbling to show the yeast have gone to work. When bubbly, add butter, 1 Tbsp rosemary, 2 cups flour, and then your salt. Stir and keep adding in flour.

2) Once your dough has come together with some rough shaping into a ball, place it in a greased/oiled bowl and cover until doubled.

3) Decide what you want to do with this dough. You can split it into two equal pieces and shape them into rounds. Set them onto a baking sheet to rise another 30-45 minutes. Alternatively, you might shape them into smaller baguette-style loaves. Pre-heat oven to 375F.

4) You can lightly oil the loaves or spritz with water before sprinkling with rosemary and sea salt.

5) Bake 20 minutes or until brown.

6) Enjoy!

3. Journalists not "Journalists"

"You have no idea what you are talking about, Luka," the small Greek colleague commented harshly and dismissively toward Luka, incensing something primal in the latter.

I had not yet met this colleague — my time as guest editor in this German newsroom left many new faces without names as I rotated through teams every couple months.

"How do you know what I have an idea about?" Luka shot back in his thickly-accented German — though I was still getting comfortable with my German language skills, he didn't sound like a native German speaker. The other members of this multicultural editorial staff shifted their eyes nervously, some chuckled, not sure what to do. I stopped moving all together, frozen in my seat at the back corner of a meeting table in a pose for observation: my posture slouched, my chin buried in my hands, my eyes fixed. A daily news discussion about refugees from Eastern Europe had escalated into a very personal conflict.

"You don't know what the refugees need. You don't know who they are, or what they are doing," the Greek colleague said, looking sure of himself, almost taunting the combustible situation toward full ignition. A soft winter light shone in through the windows behind me, and story ideas pinned to a tack board fluttered slightly.

"How dare you say I don't know," Luka growled, his tall, lanky frame rising from the table. His hands emphasized each point as his voice grew more forceful and hurt. "You don't know what it is like to leave a country as a refugee. To leave everything you know. To leave your family and friends. How dare you. I know. I lived it."

One of the more respected editors urged calm. The men shouted at each other for a few more minutes before moving to another part of the building. Someone told me Luka had been dealing with personal issues at home, probably making the discussion more than it needed to be.

The whole scene shocked and intrigued me. How, I wondered, could an issue escalate so quickly in this newsroom, and how does this passion inform journalistic practice? Was this common of all German newsrooms? How were these journalists trained to talk through issues like this? Were they trained?

Separating journalistic wheat from chaff

To become a baker in Germany, you'd need at least three years training to be taken seriously in a low-level position. As with many industries in Germany, the apprenticeship or trainee system is robust, and industry groups detail the path to your own apron on websites and in literature. Some sites even talk about celebrities who once studied to be bakers, too — it's cool to make bread!

But not *that* cool.

One HR manager told a German broadcaster that they have 10 training slots available each year for would-be bakers, but three or four of those slots are never filled. Candidates need a basic level of understanding of mathematics (interpreting and converting recipes), of technical skill to be nimble in their pretzel twisting and loaf shaping, and need to be creative in decorating or concocting bakery treats. Not every country in the European Union has the same formal training for bakers, as Germany does, meaning a German baker can boast having more formal training, perhaps, but it doesn't prevent someone from going to another country to get their baking fix.

Still, the structure and recognition for bakers in Germany is ingrained in society. With more investment of time and skill — another two or three years — a baker can get their Master Baker certificate, perhaps opening their own shop, or becoming a quality control technician, or bread sommelier. (Journalism sommeliers don't exist, though maybe they should.)

Even though Chapter 2 discussed journalism education, this detail about Germany's system can tell us something about how a society recognizes credentials and expertise.

Germany's system for valuing qualifications does apply somewhat to journalism. A chief political correspondent might have a PhD in political science, or a chief legal correspondent might be a lawyer. In these cases the subject matter of a beat is specialized, and the journalist happens to be an expert in that field.

Journalism schools do exist in Germany, but it's also possible for someone to fall into the career with enough patience, talent, and networking. Opportunities could take the form of a *Praktikum*: Internship in the American sense, with little if any pay and few responsibilities; a *Voluntariat*: A two- or three-year paid position in which one learns the trade in the hopes of eventually receiving a work contract; or a limited duration work contract. During my time working with German public media outlets, colleagues explained that the vast majority of employees are hired on these limited contracts, becoming freelancers with regular, scheduled work. These limited workers (called *feste Freie*, or regular freelancers) have little job or income security, and often work hard to prove their worth so they aren't replaced by another of the many freelancers waiting in the wings. Ultimately, the goal is to become one of the *Festangestellte*, or full-time, vested employees. Once a person achieves this stage, I was told social worker protections make it almost impossibly difficult to fire someone. The result of this job security can sometimes manifest as apathy and a massive drop-off of productivity in the newly-vested workforce.

The heavy reliance on interns and freelancers kept a precarious feeling in the air — there was a lot of turn-over and uncertainty in a place funded by the people, to serve the people. People are less likely to take risks when they have unsure footing, and reports might begin to be more self-serving because freelancers might want to pad their demo reel with something that matters to them.

At one time there was a burst of protest among the contract employees. A colleague told me about a freelancer uprising in the 1970s, during which German public media employees went to management and demanded better pay and full-time contracts, which would have created a system more akin to the U.S. model of at-will employment. The anecdote ended with freelancers never pressing their demands, leading to the entrenched system of job insecurity and fierce competition for limited roles.

Contrasted with the rigorous baker education process, it seems in Germany it's easier to work as a journalist without much formal training, or job security, than it is to walk the path toward bread sommelier.

I had just moved to a new desk and into a new office while still embedded with my German host organization. I tried to glean as much as I could from my work rotations as a guest editor: learning how meetings worked, what the process was for getting something on-air, what people do all day, and what kind of journalists these people represented.

While sitting in meetings for three hours a day — like the explosive one with Luka — I began to wonder how many of the editors had been trained in journalism, and what that training entailed. I would ask about the news values of a story, or about the use of sound in radio stories, but many editors' comments were reduced to emotional feedback or disagreements with opinions expressed in the story.

These frustrations often bled onto the daily reporter, as if the reporter manufactured the realities portrayed in the story. An example of this might be a discussion about an Italian fruit vendor facing eviction because of supply issues. The editors might use that as a way to talk for 45 minutes about the history of Italian immigrant integration issues — important, but not at all relevant to this particular story.

In my new office, at my new desk, with a new officemate, I asked for details of what is "normal" for editorial staffs. If there was a cultural or societal difference in training and expectation of professional journalists, I'd rather know sooner than later. I tried to keep an open mind, understanding that my journalism education in college and in my own radio career isn't the sum of all styles of journalism.

My colleague smirked and took a sip of water. She looked quickly at the door, and then back to me. "Why do you ask?"

"Some of the discussions we have at meetings don't feel like newsroom discussions," I said. "We don't talk about news values, or what the listeners want or need to hear. Sometimes it feels like each editor in there is an activist and only pushes their own message."

"Usually whoever is loudest wins."

"Well, not many of these editors are journalists," I remember her saying, referring to training and background. "Usually whoever is loudest wins, and their interests get on the air."

Legitimacy is in the eye of the beholder

There are plenty of people who don't fully understand the news media and the mediascape today, and the media makers are among them.

Ink-stained reporters and editors used to be the true gatekeepers of information, able to amplify or suppress stories, scandals, and secrets simply by printing information or not. That role came with great responsibility and, rightfully, scrutiny: a journalist was someone forged in a fire of institutional scrutiny (judged against and by one's peers) and public scrutiny (the ones who are supposed to be served — though recent years of the press being labeled "enemies of the people" may undercut this legacy.)

Some like to look for an easily digestible reason for leaving that inky reality in the past, but there isn't one. The advancement of the internet; the evolution of social media; the development of various forms of infotainment and commentary-as-news; the decline of newspaper subscriptions; corporate consolidation of media outlets; the reach and sophistication of corporate or government PR operations; all of this and more factor into our media reality now.

This complicated mediascape makes it difficult to define a journalist in the same way as in the past. Someone working for a legacy media organization is no longer a gatekeeper. Information is traveling at the speed of social media posts, so the defining characteristic of a "journalist" is not merely access and dissemination of information. Professional journalists are expected to have the skills necessary to more fully contextualize a story, and analyze information in a way that respects the nuance and messiness of our world. (As referenced in Chapter 1.) But that respect for nuance is not always respected itself, including from some journalists.

My time in German public media outlets was often in offices in one *Hochhaus* or another; impressive towers of glass and prestige in major city centers. Antoine was one of my officemates, who often gestured wildly while speaking any of a variety of languages. He was impressively trim, and nearly matched my 6-foot height, always dressing modestly, but professionally. His short, but neatly combed, salt-and-pepper hair and the shading of a thin mustache hid well his 60 some years of life. I mentioned Antoine to a few other colleagues, marveling at the amazing person who spoke seven languages while working on multicultural shows and reports. On the telephone he would flow seamlessly from English, to German, French, Italian, Hungarian, or Russian. Being raised in Belgium afforded him exposure to Flemish and Dutch as well.

"Who?" my colleagues asked.

"Antoine," I said. "He works with the multicultural magazine."

"Sorry. Don't know him," they all said.

It is not surprising that someone like Antoine wasn't well-known. Many of the German public radio reporters I encountered rarely mixed with other editorial staffs unless assigned to do so. Regional broadcasters might have six different stations offering 24/7 programming, so the staffing and editorial structure tended to become compartmentalized. With so many workers being free-lancers with varying schedules or assignments, getting to know everyone in one's own division can be difficult, not to mention one of the other thousands of workers in the organization.

One would think someone like Antoine should be sought after and fought over in diverse newsrooms, especially in Europe. Journalists try to learn their beats by experiencing life within a particular coverage area, but sometimes a person must turn to a wiser co-worker; someone who has visited hundreds of unique locations and speaks a half-dozen languages would have to hold indispensable worth for a listener-base craving insight and information. I mentioned once to Antoine I had considered a trip to Namibia to explore former colonial Germany. I had read the German language is still spoken by a deteriorating minority, and German place names, street signs, and history are still visible and open for observation. I had considered writing a story about the lost German colonies, and what role the German culture and subsequent world political history played on this part of the world.

"I have been there," Antoine said nonchalantly, mentioning his long-ago journey to Windhoek, Namibia's capital. "It is true German can still be found, but it is a dangerous city. Sightseeing outside of the city is great though." *He was there?!* I thought. *Of course he was.*

Someone like Antoine should be in the heart of news production, and part of a strategy to help the newsroom and the listeners build cultural literacy. I'm not sure whether or what kind of journalism training Antoine had, or how he ended up at that particular *Hochhaus* doing that particular work. But it was clear to me he was a talented journalist, and one not being used to the full benefit of his employer or the public.

One's employer alone doesn't necessarily determine whether or not they are a journalist, at least in the eyes of the law. In the United States, legal protections have been extended to the wave of journalists not working for legacy outlets. A U.S. federal appeals court in 2014, for example, ruled in a defamation case that bloggers are afforded the same First Amendment protections as professional journalists if they are writing on an issue of public concern.

A blogger had accused a court-appointed trustee and a finance company of criminally mishandling a bankruptcy case, and the trustee claimed defamation. The court said the blogger didn't show malice in the claim. The story may have been wrong, but the issue was a matter of public concern and warranted discussion.

A New Zealand High Court decision concurred in a similar case, ruling, "the definition [of who is a journalist] does not impose quality requirements and does not require the dissemination of news to be in a particular format."

In recent years there have been various offshoots of journalistic activity to different kinds of formal and informal organizations. Fact checking has become a cottage industry for example, with nonprofit, political, and even news outlets themselves creating teams of people to "fact check" claims. These "fact checkers" are subject to the same accusations of bias that any other run-of-the-mill journalist may face, resulting in a dilution of the effectiveness of "facts" being "checked," at least for me. Some communities have also formed volunteer or nonprofit citizen operations to attend and report on civic events, like city or county council meetings. While filling a need, these organizations can have varying levels of accuracy in their reporting, sometimes peppered with editorializing from the citizen, meaning a consumer of this content needs to be cautious. These examples sit apart from other initiatives for solutions journalism, civic journalism, or activist journalism, which to different degrees focus the journalistic product on a particular kind of outcome or influence.

With a broadening mediascape of people working in a journalistic capacity, and court opinions telling us that a person doesn't have to be a good journalist to be identified and protected as a journalist, where does that leave the news consumer?

Final Thoughts

Professional journalists, at least a certain breed of them, live the news and love to serve communities. Within that breed of journalist there are at least two other types: those hungry for the scoop, and mainlining breaking news; and those who want to analyze themes, and tell stories rich in characters. The common link between the two types is a sense of duty, and a pride in participating in the discourse between people and newsmakers.

But many kinds of people work in media, presenting news or information in an authoritative way, and call themselves a journalist. Some people are activists or advocates with clear biases, and they use journalism as a means to an end. Some people are merely propagandists who spread gossip or falsehoods for monetary, political, or personal gain. Some people share information as a hobby: organizations like Bellingcat and members of the burgeoning open source intelligence community combine publicly available data, social media posts, and citizen analysis to investigate the realities of conflict and war, independent of official information channels.

All of these people can be considered journalists, but the bigger question is: should they be? News consumers and news producers alike should take care in the labels we give, and the news sources we endorse and support. There is a difference in expectation between a professional journalist from *The New York Times*, and a citizen journalist on Facebook, Twitter, or any other social media platform. Both can be called journalists, but we may intellectually expect very different products from the two. How can we distinguish what we're getting, and what we want to get?

There's no easy answer to the question: who is a journalist? Everyone can be one, but that doesn't do justice to the skills, loyalties, and general expectations (positive or negative) the public has when that title is given. News consumers have to vet the media outlets, and the people producing the news, to figure out where on the great spectrum of journalistic quality any given publication lies. On one end of the spectrum might be a propagandist, and on the other end a journalism sommelier. We can use the term "journalist" for both, but there's a great chasm between definitions.

Let's advocate for more sommeliers, and fewer propagandists.

Bake Bread: Irish Gingerbread

Is a quick-bread even a bread, or is it just cake? Here's a nice treat, Irish Gingerbread as made by Tony Ganzer.

1) Add all dry ingredients, except oatmeal, in a small bowl. Put sugar and butter in a larger bowl, and begin to whip them into a smooth mix.

2) Mix in eggs, and molasses, in the larger bowl. Try to make the mix as smooth as possible without chunks of butter or sugar.

3) Mix in half of the dry ingredients. Once well mixed, add the other half of the dry ingredients.

4) Mix in oats and warm water. Mix it well!

5) Pre-heat oven to 350F. Pour the mixture into a very well-greased bread pan. A 5×9 baking pan works, but a 9 inch square might work, too.

6) Bake 40-45 minutes until a toothpick comes out clean from the center of the bread. You might check on the bread after 30 minutes.

7) Enjoy!

4. Media, Machiavelli, and Power

Niccolò Machiavelli wrote about power and people by candlelight at his estate outside Florence in 1520, maybe with hints of wild rosemary and other regional flora in the air. One could imagine typical night sounds which may have played soundtrack to his political analysis, with the braying and chirping of a countryside untouched by endless push alerts of *ultime notizie* (breaking news.) His estate remained unsullied by the eternal wails of pundits and sound bytes which seem to drive our modern conversations and musings.

Machiavelli had his own form of media and matter to consume to be sure, amid the ruthless jockeying of regional leaders each attempting to position his fiefdom as the most formidable. The parsing of arguments in tracts and literature — maybe generously seasoned with a slanderous claim or two — is a far cry from our modern mediascape that puts a premium on immediacy and exclusivity instead of comprehensiveness and nuance.

It seems reasonable to think Machiavelli's *The Prince* may have had another chapter or two if Fox News or MSNBC followed the machinations of Renaissance politicking as thoroughly as that of our world now.

Even without those chapters, Machiavelli's recognition of what it takes to find and keep power may teach us something amid heated skirmishes in the modern "War on Media." Assaults on the Fourth Estate may not equate to the feuding principalities of Italy's past, but that doesn't mean a brief thought exercise isn't helpful.

Niccolò Machiavelli wrote about power and people at his estate outside Florence.

Machiavelli's reputation has taken hits over the centuries, and many scholars say it's undeserved. He was a diplomat, a student of politics in his time, and an analyst of power's influence and reach from many perspectives. Noted author and political philosopher Erica Benner summarized Machiavelli as being "convinced the real threats to freedom come from within — from gross inequalities on the one hand, and extreme partisanship on the other. He saw first-hand that authoritarian rule can take root and flourish in such conditions with terrifying ease."

That assessment is likely different than the reputation Machiavelli holds in your head. His name often conjures thoughts of being ruthless and calculating while preserving and amassing power. This impression is not all together inappropriate given the cold realities of Machiavelli's time.

A man (and bread) of his time

While Machiavelli studied power from Florence, neighboring fiefdoms experienced their own power struggles with political players built and destroyed with the shifting weather. But not all dynasties were so fleeting. To the northeast, in Ferrara, members of the house of Este ruled from the 13th to 16th centuries until the city was put under direct papal rule, after a dispute over succession. The Estensi in their prime held out-sized influence in Italian politics and established Ferrara as a cultural and artistic hub, including for food.

The chef for the house of Este until his death in 1548, Cristoforo di Messisbugo, penned a masterpiece of Renaissance culinary literature with recipes and banquet instructions. *Banchetti, Composizioni di Vivande e Apparecchio Generale* (Banquets, Dish Compositions/ Recipes and General Presentation) provided a guide for creating banquets worthy of princes who work up an appetite during the machinations of the 16th century everyday.

One such item mentioned by Messisbugo is the *coppia ferrarese*, a twisted bread that looks like multiple bread-sticks have united to form the arms and legs of a dough-person without any head. While this may seem like a fitting treat in a ruthless political environment, one report says the coppia was actually formed for a carnival dinner in 1536 to resemble the curls of a noblewoman of the time. Its legacy has stretched far beyond that dinner. The coppia now holds DOP status: *Denominazione d' Origine Protetta*, a protected status for EU goods from specific geographic regions.

Italy during the Renaissance seems to blend a kind of enlightened recognition of beauty, art, and creation, with devastating political intrigue. Shortly after the house of Este had become a shell of its former self, a biographical entry of a descendant describes him as "inclined toward treachery in politics, [but] he gave art his patronage."

Treachery and patronage: two words with a timeless nature that might be used to describe aspects of politics in our own time, just as it might for the politics of the Estensi or the Florentine house of Medici, where Machiavelli observed the world just three or four days away by horseback.

The certain level of timelessness for Machiavelli's obser-
vations in *The Prince* stems from the fact that his views
on political maneuvering, at their core, are about human
nature in cutthroat — sometimes literally — power
dynamics. Take this line on optics and political imaging:
"Everyone sees what you appear to be, few really know
what you are." In another line that seems ripped from
modern headlines, Machiavelli said hatred breeds con-
spiracies, but a conspirator lacking popular support "...has
the people for an enemy, and thus cannot hope for any
escape."

Time and time again Machiavelli warns against losing the
people, because rule and influence rest on whether it's
popular support or suspicion forming the threads holding
Damocles' sword. "The best possible fortress is not to be
hated by the people," he writes.

There are many historical instances of treating the press
as an *enemy of the people*, but the escalating political
rhetoric in our modern "War on Media" set my mind to
Machiavelli right away. With historical examples from
Nazi Germany, and Stalin's Soviet Union, among others,
the label *enemy of the people* has stoked visceral antag-
onism and discrimination of opponents of brutal, auto-
cratic regimes.

It's why U.S. President Donald Trump's use of the phrase piqued interest and concern among journalists and observers. In a 2017 tweet, Trump said, "The FAKE NEWS media (failing @nytimes, @NBCNews, @ABC, @CBS, @CNN) is not my enemy, it is the enemy of the American People!" Trump repeated his use of the phrase on other occasions, sometimes clarifying he was directing it at purveyors of fake news — news known to be false or fabricated — but later used the term to refer to outlets he saw as critical of or opposing him.

For people in power, their position is safer if they have control over as much as possible: control over the message; control over the medium; control over the labels of friend and foe. Machiavelli knew this, of course, writing, "a wise prince should establish himself on that which is in his own control and not that of others."

Machiavelli said that people are fickle, ungrateful, and false, so keeping power rests largely in controlling as much of a situation as possible. Relying on fate or luck is a fool's errand. And connecting this idea to media, we see that a free press is a dangerous variable in a quest to maximize political power.

True power of the press

Journalists, at their core, are supposed to be representatives for their fellow citizens. They're afforded a Willy

Wonka-style "golden ticket" to enter board rooms, factory floors, and the streets of our communities to show and help explain what is really going on. A free press has immense power in a society, because it's an unrestrained and committed advocate for a just and efficient society. It's a tool of accountability and record. It's a tool of reflection and analysis.

Or at least it has the potential to fill that role.

The power of the press is really about the power of the people, because the press is providing the people with information needed to pressure leaders. The press can't fine someone. The press can't legally sanction someone in a court. The press can't imprison someone. But the press can ask questions, and frame situations for the public. This might be seen as wresting control of the public conversation away from a nervous "prince."

It's the public, and institutions formed by and serving them, that mete out punishment sometimes based on reporting, but the press can only inform. As revered journalist Bill Moyers wrote, "the First Amendment is the first for a reason. It's needed to keep our leaders honest and to arm the powerless with the information they need to protect themselves against the tyranny of the powerful, whether that tyranny is political or commercial."

There is no monolithic *media* acting with one brain and motivation. This may seem to not be true given that many media organizations appear to follow the same stories, narratives, and people day in and day out.

Still, many people generally understand that the press, even in an idealized view, should be a servant to society, and it's in the interest of power-hungry "princes" to undermine that covenant. One of the oft-repeated maxims of Machiavelli is that for a leader it is better to be feared than loved. Gratitude doesn't safeguard power as effectively as if a leader strikes terror.

Machiavelli though prefaced that section by saying if there's an option, try to be *both* loved and feared. But most importantly, in my view:

> "A *prince ought to inspire fear in such a way that, if he does not win love, he avoids hatred.*"

You can't maintain power, at least in the long run, if you're universally despised, hated, or reviled. This is meant to act as an observation for politicians, but what if it can be turned into a tactic? What if demonizing the free press, and stoking hatred of it, are efforts to undermine that covenant with the public? If the press isn't trusted, then its information and analysis aren't influencing the public or institutions as intended. Power can be better consolidated without the scrutiny; more of the situation can be controlled.

Dirty Press

What if the press itself is being Machiavellian, and it's brought this war on itself?

Some years ago a book called *The Princely Press* imagined Machiavelli in an interview about American journalism. The Fake Machiavelli talks mostly about journalists who may be seeking individual glory, and might adopt unethical tactics to get scoops and fame.

The means are less important than the end, in Machiavelli's world.

The press "must not permit itself to be weakened by those in the public who call for a more democratic, community-minded, and socially responsible media system," Fake Machiavelli said. "The press must assume its princely status."

There *are* journalists and information agents (as I call them) who are serving themselves more than the public, and use any means necessary to get a scoop which will get them glory. The same impulse may drive journalists to create fictitious sources, facts, or events to build up the perceived exclusivity or value of a report. The sagas of Jayson Blair or Stephen Glass act as cautionary tales in journalistic fabrication and plagiarism which contributed to an erosion of trust for the industry at-large (not to mention derailing their careers and becoming fodder for journalism ethicists.) The visibility of fraudsters or opportunists among the ranks of journalists may be greater in the digital age, but their numbers are incredibly small when viewed against the entire mediascape. Instead, it is the misuse or cheapening of the power of the press, by the press, that may be a greater threat than hubris.

"*A prince ought to inspire fear in such a way that, if he does not win love, he avoids hatred.*"

Take the media's promotion of and collaboration with the pundit class, and the ever-freer granting of source anonymity as two examples of a squandering of journalistic power and responsibility.

The news ecosystem is ever more hectic, and a social media post can change the course of the national political, economic, and social agenda in a flash. Our age is one where the spread of details of a self-immolation of a street vendor can push a country like Tunisia closer to revolution, or video of excessive use of force and brutality by police or security forces can fuel international calls and protests for racial justice and human rights protections. In between the moments of tweet-driven outrage, however, media outlets still feel the need to keep their cable shows, websites, Facebook Lives, etc., fresh, interesting, and relevant. The competition for eyeballs and advertisers is fierce, so it makes sense, from a business perspective, that networks would want to have experts on retainer to fill that time. This gets us to the enabling of the hired pundit class, whose opinions are used to fuel a cycle of reaction, hypothesis, and knee-jerk analysis for the audience's entertainment (and presumably education?)

Critics have long called this *checkbook journalism*: paying for a story, analysis, or insight. While the producer may have someone to fill time at their every beck and call, the audience is left wondering whether the guest's motives are pure. Journalists are to seek out the right sources, experts, industry analysts, characters, etc. to help explain a news story. Those voices are included to add context and build public understanding, with the compensation for that contribution — if you want to call it compensation — being notoriety, validation, and maybe added respect in the wider public. But if you introduce money to the equation, the audience could wonder whether the "expertise" is fabricated just so the person can get paid. Maybe the guest knows that saying something sensational will keep the gravy train rolling, so they gauge their appearances accordingly. This can taint the news product, and make an already skeptical public more skeptical about exactly why someone is saying something about something, and for how much money are they doing it.

A piece from *Slate* noted in 1998 that such checkbook compensation for television "depends primarily on whether the particular TV show is classified as "entertainment" or "news." You might expect the guests on farcical programs hosted by Jerry Springer or Maury Povich to get an all-expenses-paid trip to better facilitate the spectacle of conflict or scandal. Network TV shows like Good Morning America, or The Today Show, have also been known to cut checks for certain material, but these shows are hybrid news/entertainment programs, creating at least a perception of ambiguity in journalistic integrity.

But punditry is something different. After the second war in Iraq, the *American Journalism Review* (AJR) revisited the pundit issue, with the rise of military experts explaining the ins-and-outs of a polarizing war. Cable and legacy networks wanted to have the best analysis from the highest-ranking military officers possible. "Exclusivity is one of the goals," a spokeswoman for ABC News told AJR at the time. Programs, publications, or networks often strive for that exclusivity by booking newsmakers to give high-level analysis and insight, which stands as a journalistic product on its own.

The result of this pundit arms race has been a noisy reality in which our screens are increasingly filled with opinions-as-analysis not out of any real motive to decode our complicated world. All too often audiences aren't being bombarded with high-quality information, rather they're given political sniping, speculation, or manufactured controversy as *news*. To borrow from von Clausewitz: news punditry is not only an extension of politics by other means, but increasingly an end in itself. This has promoted a din of anger and watered-down conversation packaged as something exclusive.

Journalism's credibility and overall influence is also undermined by the misuse or abuse of certain tools in the journalist's toolbox, like anonymity. It used to be an exception to grant anonymity to sources offering some unattainable insight, intentionally-hidden fact, or testimony given at grave risk to personal safety. But increasingly the exception seems to be more of a norm.

If and when to grant anonymity is one of the more controversial discussions in the journalism realm, and it should be. A written, broadcast, tweeted, Instagrammed, or otherwise disseminated story or claim needs to carry credibility and provability, lest a modern "prince" accuses one of creating "fake news." At the same time, the eternal news cycle has led some journalists to seek big stories on tighter deadlines, and has led some sources to fear being pilloried by online trolls and legitimate critics alike.

Time pressure and stress to find sources, combined with source reticence to face the trolls, has led to looser controls on anonymity.

In September 2018, *The New York Times* just about broke the internet when it published an unsigned opinion piece from someone who claimed to "work for the president but like-minded colleagues and I have vowed to thwart parts of his agenda and his worst inclinations."

The piece "I Am Part of the Resistance Inside the Trump Administration" instantly drew condemnation and support that crossed ideological and journalistic lines. *The Times* knew publishing an anonymous opinion piece of this magnitude demanded an explanation, and would attract criticism. The editor's note at the top of the unsigned item said they believed anonymity was provided because it was the only way to provide readers with an important perspective. Maybe, or maybe not. The anonymous author parlayed the experience into a book deal, before going public with his identity to CNN. The author, former Trump administration official Miles Taylor, then became a CNN contributor, and joined the pundit class.

Confidentiality and trust are the coins of the journalistic realm, and to inform the public, journalists need to be able to inform themselves. But we are no longer in a time when a journalist's word is enough — they need to be held accountable to themselves, their audience, and their communities. Transparency serves accountability, and journalists can knock down slanderous claims against their reporting by showing their work and methods, and more often than not naming the sources making claims. Anonymity serves a purpose, but shouldn't be granted just because someone doesn't want to face the consequences of spreading gossip.

The Society of Professional Journalists gives two pointed thoughts:

1. **Identify sources whenever feasible. The public is entitled to as much information as possible on sources' reliability.**
2. **Always question sources' motives before promising anonymity. Clarify conditions attached to any promise made in exchange for information. Keep promises.**

News outlets have robust editorial hierarchies in place — and in some ways *The Times* represents journalism's best-of-the-best — but those hierarchies don't mean much to huge segments of the population that are anti-*media* or generally journalist-averse. Putting faceless or nameless persons in news stories is perpetuating the internet-age culture of no accountability in the anonymous criticisms lobbed from near and far.

Journalists at one time, and still today, spoke with anonymous sources on background (not for quoting or recording), and used that insight to guide them to people who would go on the record, or documents that show the record. But those anonymous persons are now the ones showing up in the stories, in some cases without the paper trail to follow.

Even with the risk of backlash for sources sharing opinions on sensitive topics, journalists need not cheapen this tool of granting anonymity. The press can't build or regain trust from a public that is ever more skeptical of the news by failing to find flesh-and-blood people to go on the record. Some stories demand anonymity to protect someone's life, to protect a national security secret, and the like. And the sources demand that protection. But those cases are somewhat rare, and granting anonymity should be, too.

If journalists don't assume their role as an advocate for the people, and preserve their tools and profession for that end, outside normal political sniping, then journalism is reduced to just another fiefdom approaching collapse.

Final Thoughts

Journalism, in the best circumstances, is a tool to help preserve a balance of power in a society between the public and those ruling with the consent of the governed. Places which lack basic constitutional freedoms may not share this reality or prospect, at least in the short-term, but the amassing and preserving of power is still at stake and at play.

Information can breathe insight into a populace hungry for life, liberty, and a pursuit of happiness, and this supports the idea of information being a source of power.

The direct manipulation of information, and a press which might distribute it, is thus a way to foster distrust and quell tools of accountability. That distrust is also fueled by conspiracy theories, bot networks flooding social media with falsehoods, and any number of media methods deployed to promote fiction over reality. Ruthless or selfish behavior among journalists compounds the collateral damage in the "war on media" by undermining the place of true power for the press: the ability to hold the trust, attention, and protection of the public. Information can fuel dissent and division, or unity and community, depending on how it's shared and contextualized. The stakes of the information influence game are high.

High too are the stakes related to the politics of bread, which can lead to rebellion, as demonstrated in France in Chapter 1, and Egypt in Chapter 5. The manipulation of one of life's necessities has long been exploited by rulers to keep a hold on power. Long before Machiavelli's time, Roman coins in the first century held an image of Caesar on one side and the agriculture goddess of Ceres on the other side, holding a stalk of wheat. (Ceres leads us to "cereal.") An article from Getty, a cultural and philanthropic institution, said this pairing of imagery was to remind the people of the generosity of emperors who subsidized wheat/bread costs. One could imagine wheat prices being topic of conversation at Roman community ovens or bakeries, and how much more fruitful might those conversations have been with fuller context provided by journalism.

In any age, efforts to stir hatred of the press are meant to undermine the relationship between audience and journalists, and lessen the resources for and sting of reports meant to help us understand our communities and institutions better. The press is not beyond reproach, and its failings should be addressed honestly in a measured way. But the role of the free press is vital to a vibrant, informed, and functioning democracy. Preserving its integrity is of systemic concern.

So amid bluster, aggression, and destructive language targeting *the media*, I offer a final, cherry-picked quote from *The Prince*: "Proceed in a temperate manner with prudence and humanity..."

Bake Bread: Rosemary Asiago

A bread for an appetizer, or as a hearty companion to a soup perhaps. You could also just enjoy it as a meal in itself!

You need:

Warm water: 1 cup
Active dry yeast: 2.5 tsp
Olive oil: 1/4 cup
Salt: 1/2 tsp
Black pepper: 1 Tbsp
Rosemary: 1 Tbsp
Flour: 3 1/4 cup
Asiago cheese (shredded): 1.5 cups

1) Mix sugar, yeast, and warm water in a bowl. Begin to stir, waiting for bubbling to show the yeast have gone to work. Then, add olive oil, salt, rosemary, pepper, and flour. Stir and add in flour as necessary.

2) On a lightly floured surface, begin kneading, and add flour if it's too sticky – but not too much! Work in 1 cup of cheese as you knead.

3) Grease a second bowl, and let your dough rest in a warm spot until doubled. It could take a bit of time...

4) Punch down dough, split, and shape it into two round loaves, or keep it as one big loaf if you like. You can also shape the dough into 75-90 gram rolls. Set them on a greased/oiled pan. Let rise for about 30 minutes. Spritz with water and sprinkle cheese on top!

5) Pre-heat oven to 425F.

6) Bake 30-35 minutes until brown. Rolls will likely only take 18-20 minutes.

7) Enjoy!

5. Bread diplomacy and Egyptian revolution

With equal parts skill and courage — or carelessness — our Cairo taxi driver weaved in and out of mystifying traffic patterns on the way to Giza.

"He wants to know where you're from," Hamed turned to me in the back seat, breaking from the small-talk in Arabic with the driver. The curious thing about traveling during a revolution is you're not quite sure what is real and who can be trusted. Adding a language barrier to the political instability can leave you a bit disoriented and paranoid.

"Really?" I made a quick calculation of how I thought the rest of the long ride across the city would go if I said I'm an American. "Just tell him I work for Swiss radio."

Although I told the truth, Hamed gave me a puzzled look at first. But then he understood.

"Ah, you're probably right, that's best," he said.

It's not that there was a great danger identifying my nationality, but conversations about America can quickly turn to conversations about American foreign policy, and depending on the part of the world you're in, that conversation might just as quickly turn contentious. I've had many of those conversations in years living abroad and in reporting on immigration and asylum policy. Usually I tried to build bridges and dispel misconceptions as best I could, but during this reporting trip a year after the transformative popular protests in and beyond Tahrir Square, it didn't seem to be a time to jump into random conversations on long cab rides, through an interpreter.

One source of my caution rested in a fundamental lack of understanding of the nuances of journalism in Egypt. There is no universal reality for news reporting around the world as the norms, laws, risks, and benefits of journalism depend a lot on the context of the place or event being covered. It's why "parachute journalism" is dangerous, so named because foreign reporters might descend on a country for a big scoop just as paratroopers might precede a full-scale assault. These journalists may have little-to-no expertise on the story or region, and rely on fixers on the ground to decode the situation. These fixers might be local journalists or tour guides who need extra money.

I didn't want to be seen as a parachutist when I agreed to travel to Cairo with Hamed in February 2012, during a still turbulent period after the ouster of long-time strongman Hosni Mubarak. Hamed worked as an intervention specialist in Zurich: kind of a mix between a social worker and goodwill ambassador for social services. I met him while reporting a story on homelessness in Zurich, and managed to earn his trust to learn more of his personal story. ("You have honest eyes," Hamed told me.) Over an evening of open conversation and a careful ride-along with Hamed and his colleague, I ultimately earned an invite to join him on a visit to a still evolving post-revolutionary reality of his hometown.

The curious thing about traveling during a revolution is you're not quite sure what is real and who can be trusted.

It may seem strange to a non-journalist that I might be willing to travel with someone I just met to a country with a tenuous political situation. I'm not an expert on Egyptian politics or history, and at the time of this trip I hadn't yet completed my graduate studies that were heavily influenced by the so-called Arab Uprisings. Maybe it *was* strange. But after weeks of interviewing members of the Egyptian diaspora in Zurich, and learning more about Hamed, a Swiss-Egyptian view of Egypt's political evolution seemed like a story that needed to be told.

Egyptian bread is life

The Egyptian dialect of Arabic has a word that can be used for both "bread" and "life:" *aish*. Following World War II, the Egyptian state subsidized household staples like bread and sugar. The World Bank in 2019 said about 60% of Egypt's population was considered poor or vulnerable amid increasing inequality. In light of this, access to low-cost *baladi*, peasant flat bread, might literally mean life or death.

Subsidies also acted as a countermeasure to potential civil unrest through regime changes and economic instability. This was the case after the military overthrow in 1952 of the Egyptian King Farouk by Gamal Abdel Nasser and his allies, who relied on state subsidies to buy legitimacy and peace as they created the basis for a socialist economy. One analysis of U.S. foreign food shipments found Egypt was the world's largest per capita consumer of American food aid by 1963, with wheat (flour) being a key ingredient.

The problem with subsidized bread is many-fold, not least of which is that if a government is using cheap bread to keep the peace, then an increase of bread prices will increase the risk of unrest. Under Anwar Sadat, the Egyptian government's attempts to change the cheap bread status quo prompted civilian rebellion, leading to the bread uprising of 1977. The reason for the change is tied to Egypt's foreign debt, reliance on foreign wheat, poor domestic harvests, and international pressure for a more liberalized economy — all things that don't much matter to citizens who battle hunger and economic uncertainty with regularity.

Another problem with subsidies is that they can foster economic and political corruption. If the state is subsidizing access to cheaper flour for bakers to make cheaper bread for citizens, then it's only a matter of time before enterprising middlemen try to buy up the cheap stuff and sell it at a mark-up on the black market, or just skim a bit off the top. Amid skyrocketing wheat prices in 2008, Egyptian bakeries saw disruptions from desperate citizens, rebelling against increasingly difficult access to life's necessities in the form of 160 gram loaves of *baladi*. A government bakery inspector told *The New York Times* that, "the most corrupt sector in the country is the provisions sector," and then proceeded to explain how bribes could work for falsifying subsidized flour compliance records. If everyone is skimming a little off the top and the bottom of your piece of *aish*, are you left with much of a life to live?

Bread uprisings then might be seen as a direct result of a population out of options in a dysfunctional system. The English historian, activist, and Marxist E.P. Thompson wrote of Britain's experience that, "It is of course true that riots were triggered off by soaring prices, by malpractices among dealers, or by hunger. But these grievances operated within a popular consensus as to what were legitimate and what were illegitimate practices in marketing, milling, baking, etc." One could interpret this as recognition of the social contract between governor and governed, and the expectations for the services and conditions provided to everyone in society.

One might also see parallels in the concept of *dimuqratiyyat al-khubz*, which the Tunisian writer and political science professor Larbi Sadiki says means "democracy of bread" in Arabic. In this phrase we're given another word for "bread" (*khubz*) which can be used more generally for items provided by a state in exchange for relative social acceptance for a regime. "Essentially, its chief premise is that post-independence Arab rulers have been paid political deference by their peoples in return for the provision of publicly subsidized services: education, health care, and a state commitment to securing employment. Hence political deference has been traded off for *khubz*," Sadiki writes. "Arab authoritarianism has not reproduced itself solely by relying on brute force, but also on 'elements of negotiation and accommodation.'" Under such a form of authoritarianism, the public may not have certain constitutional liberties like freedom of press, expression, property, or judicial independence, but they are supplied with certain necessities. If the bread — either literally or figuratively in the form of government provision — stops coming, then the covenant is broken.

Bread, in this scenario, equates to power and peace.

Pyramids and the public toilet

Out of the tightly layered rows of dusty buildings from Cairo's core, the Great Pyramid of Giza springs from the desert like the wonder it is. Driving southwest of my hotel near Tahrir Square — the site of the 2011 demonstrations and heart of the revolution — Hamed and I found ourselves at the gates of the Sphinx and pyramids that hold mythic significance for Egypt, the world, and for Hamed personally. He and I traveled to visit his mother in her rooftop home just steps from Tahrir Square, and to Hamed's old haunts throughout downtown Cairo to gauge what had changed post-revolution. He told me the pyramids played a role in his younger years, seeing him go into the desert and build a fire to grill food and take in life. This seemed like a place worth visiting, and for gathering some of his thoughts on tape for my radio series.

I didn't know what to expect when coming to Egypt, so I carried all of my most important equipment on me at all times. I hid memory cards in my hotel room when I was out doing interviews, but never left behind my audio recorder, microphone, or press pass from the Egyptian government. After the fall of Mubarak, the government seemed to be running on bureaucratic momentum and military oversight. Although policemen were stationed around the city, the military held the true power, and I was advised by a number of people not to draw attention to myself as I produced my series. I had to explain to a government official that I was not in the country to ask random Egyptians about their political situation, rather just to profile Hamed and interview other Swiss officials as time allowed. After a long morning waiting in a government office fortified by machine gun nests, I also made clear I was not there to take video for television broadcast.

The pyramids seemed one of the safer stops on my trip, given how many tourists visit there, and how many plain-clothes police and government officials were milling about. Hamed and I had already walked through a market-place offering illicit knives and stun guns (which would've earned you jail time before the revolution, Hamed said), and we had seen roving protests through darkened streets while I tried to keep my recording equipment out of sight. The pyramids, in the daytime, didn't carry the same kind of stress.

I walked with Hamed to the entrance window and bought us tickets, before moving into a security checkpoint. Men with assault rifles stood around an older x-ray machine. I put my backpack on the conveyor and watched it enter the machine. A second later men started shouting, and moving quickly — obviously something was wrong, and my bag was the problem. Hamed explained that the guards thought I had camera equipment, which was not allowed without a permit that cost thousands of dollars. We were escorted out of the checkpoint and I was told I wouldn't be allowed in with my recorder.

Interviewing Hamed at the pyramids was not vital to my profile of him, but if I'm already in Cairo and this place reflects a part of his pre-revolutionary life, I thought the experience was worth trying. We stood outside the ticket counter, weighing our options.

"How about paying money to these guys? Does that work?" I asked. It's not that I thought the guards could be bought, but in my short time in Cairo I had found that some extra Egyptian pounds tended to smooth the path for everything from transportation to museum rules on digital (still) cameras.

"No, not these guys. That won't work," Hamed said, looking a little annoyed by the roadblock to our entry.

"How about we find the guy in charge and just tell him what's going on? Who's *The Guy* here?" I asked Hamed, earning myself a look that might be described as bemusement and disbelief.

"What?! That's not what happens here," Hamed was clearly confused.

"Yeah, maybe. But how about you ask one of these plain-clothes officials about it, and say I'm a foreign journalist who doesn't know anything. Maybe we get lucky."

Hamed wasn't convinced, but to his credit he walked to some of the guys we presumed were officials, based on their choice of jeans, (faux) leather jackets, and all-around demeanor. I saw them glancing back at me, and though I don't speak Arabic I can imagine the conversation contained a lot of, "this guy doesn't know what he's talking about," and, "I'm sorry, I know he is clearly naive."

"Okay, it's that guy over there," Hamed said after his huddle, pointing to an older man sitting near a public toilet. We made our way to the man, drinking tea and reading a newspaper, who was, if I remember right, an official with the culture ministry. I smiled as Hamed began speaking to the man, trying to look as non-threatening as possible.

The man seemed confused, but ultimately unbothered as he answered Hamed.

"I can't believe it: he said it's fine. We need to have someone stay with us, though." Hamed's befuddlement had only grown through this exchange, but it seemed like he was impressed in some way. We walked back to the security checkpoint and one of the men with what looked like an AK-47 walked with us through doors taking us toward the pyramids. About halfway up a trail toward the pyramid the guard stopped suddenly, clearly upset, and began ushering us back to the checkpoint.

"Hamed, what now?!" I asked.

"He's saying he can't do this, that this is wrong, and he has a family," Hamed explained, though I still didn't understand. "It will be okay though." We continued with the guard to the public toilet and the man with the tea and newspaper. After some discussion, Hamed looked at me.

"Okay. You're going to give your backpack to this guy, who is going to keep it in the bathroom," Hamed said, gesturing to an older man who I assume acts as an attendant for the bathroom.

"What?! Why am I giving this guy my backpack?!" I asked, trying not to show displeasure as much as disbelief.

"It will be okay, nothing will happen to it. It's a Muslim thing." Hamed said, though I'm filled with questions. I bent down and removed the memory cards from my recorder and take a quick inventory of what's in my bag, thinking

I may never see it again. I had made copies of all of my interviews up to this point, and only had a few "nice to have" interviews left in my trip. If I had to modify plans because of this random visit to a public toilet, so be it.

Guards escorted Hamed and me back to the checkpoint before letting us through to the pyramids alone. Despite my bag now firmly out of my hands, I still had a job to do. In my pocket was my iPhone 3GS with an audio recording app, and in my coat was my digital (still) camera, allowing me to conduct interviews as planned. After experiencing the site through Hamed's memories and reflections, we made our way back to the public toilet. The main toilet attendant and a number of plainclothes officials stood there as we walked up.

The attendant called to a younger man who then hurriedly ran into the bathroom. He ran out with a big garbage bag, which he put on the ground at my feet. He ripped open the garbage bag to reveal another garbage bag, which he again ripped open to reveal my backpack.

"You need to check it and make sure it's okay," Hamed said. I bent down and realized everyone was watching me intently, and no one was smiling. The face of the bathroom attendant looked fearful and worried, maybe even a little terrified. I checked for two things in the backpack: the main audio recorder and the microphone, worth hundreds of dollars. I looked up and smiled at everyone.

We were escorted out of the checkpoint and I was told I wouldn't be allowed in with my recorder.

"It's great, thank you so much! Thank you!" I said, trying to give the biggest smile and head nod I could to show gratitude.

"Now you need to give this man some money," Hamed said, referring to the attendant who now looked relieved. I pulled out some money — I don't remember how much — and gave it to him. I had also packed some mini Swiss chocolates as an ice breaker for the trip, and offered everyone (attendant, officials, Hamed) as much as they wanted. The smiles continued as Hamed told me we should get out of there as quickly as possible.

What's old is new again

Egyptian unrest and discontent in 2008 was prompted by spiking commodity prices, poverty, and hunger, but did not yet spiral into a revolution. From one lens it could be seen as a natural reaction in the cycle of subsidy, protest, and political appeasement. A review of grain riots during the Mamluk sultanate (years 1250-1517) by Boaz Shoshan revealed familiar realities to those seen in modern times. There's evidence leaders delivered bread to poor residents of Cairo in 1416. Sultans also employed market inspectors to enforce price regulations for grain. The weight of bread loaves may have been regulated as well, though standardized measurements may not have always been observed during periods of grain scarcity. In 1394 some Cairo residents complained to a "vice sultan" about grain prices, blaming the inspector for driving up costs while throwing stones at him. The ruler ordered an investigation of millers and grain brokers, and ordered grain reserves to be sold to hungry residents or be subjected to looting. Shoshan said this appears to be tacit approval of plunder of grain if owners didn't obey, leading eventually to a tendency of the crowds to take up stones when the grain situation didn't seem aboveboard.

In 2010 and 2011, drought and wildfires in Russia contributed to a spike in the price and availability of grain. Then prime minister Vladimir Putin banned grain exports amid what was dubbed the worst drought in more than a century, strangling supply for an importer like Egypt. As food prices and inflation rose, Mubarak's government couldn't impose subsidies big enough to counter global events. Hunger, and dissatisfaction with a dysfunctional system that was seen as no longer supplying literal or figurative bread to the people, prompted Egyptians to take up their own stones while demanding a better life, and trying to redefine expectations in civil society.

During my time in Cairo I interviewed Khaled Fahmy, then chair of the history department at the American University of Cairo, about the significance of the revolution from a physical and philosophical standpoint. With the years of subsidies and dysfunction came curbs on certain freedoms, including to gather and engage openly:

> "They cut off trees that gave shade; they put very slippery marble tiles that made it very difficult to walk in the square on the sidewalk; and then they erected these very, very thick and high fences that prevent people from crossing streets, supposedly for safety, but in fact, and this is in all big squares in Cairo, there was a deliberate attempt, and it doesn't take a genius to find this out, to prevent people from congregating [...] People are now feeling that the country belongs to them, and that's not to be taken for granted [...] The amount

of conversations, and deliberations, and very, very serious political debates that took place in Tahrir over the last 13 months now, is something Egypt has not witnessed in 60 years."

Part of this reclamation of the country was seen in Egyptian media habits before, during, and after the revolution. An analysis by journalism professors Sadaf Ali and Shahira Fahmy points to the growth of Facebook use in Egypt during the 2011 protests as showing a circumventing of tightly controlled media channels, increasing 29 percent compared to 12 percent the year before. Social media became a store for real-time documentation of protest, oppression, and organization during a dynamic period. Before I traveled to Cairo with Hamed, I followed dozens of Twitter accounts of Egyptians who provided in English a status report of unrest, political organization, and even calls for aid during clashes with security forces in Tahrir Square. Social media helped fuel organized protest across the region during the so-called Arab Uprisings, but Egypt's deposition of Mubarak seemed for a time to be an opportunity to correct social and economic imbalance. And freedom of expression, and of the media, seemed to be taking root with the potential to bloom.

When Mohamed Morsi and the Muslim Brotherhood won power in 2012, some observers were cautiously optimistic for what change may come, even incrementally. One report in *Egypt Today* described Morsi as thinking, "he would satisfy people by promising them to solve problems concerning fuel, traffic, security and bread in 100 days."

But those grand goals ran into a number of hurdles previously not faced in an authoritarian system. "Morsi was considered the first president to come in power by a real democratic process. He was the first president to be censured and mocked by almost all private newspapers in various journalistic forms, including opinion articles and even news, without the fear of being punished by authorities," the report continued.

Some of the satire against Morsi came in the form of a heart surgeon-turned-comedian Bassem Youssef, who created a program modeled after The Daily Show by Jon Stewart. The existence of a program devoted to pillorying politicians may seem nothing of note to countries with a tradition of freedom of expression, but in Egypt there was an audience ready for it.

Rulers were not.

Youssef faced investigations under Morsi's tenure, with pressure only growing after Morsi was ousted in a landslide election of former general Abdel Fattah al-Sisi. With the perceived resumption of power by the military, Youssef ultimately felt forced to end his program. "For the millionth time, I say this is supposed to be a comedy show. I am not a fighter or a warrior. I was just expressing my views once a week ... but honestly, I am tired of struggling and worrying about my safety and that of my family," he said at the time.

Fearing arrest, Youssef left Egypt for the United States, and with him a visible sign that the public square had been in the hands of the people, at least for a time.

Hamed and I hurried away from the officials and bathroom attendant, walking with a purpose to nearby taxi cabs. I was thankful I still had my gear and the interaction with officials seemed to be a success, but I also still carried with me a combined sense of vigilance and unease. We approached a cab and Hamed opened the front passenger door, as I moved to open the back door.

"No, don't get in yet," he said. The driver, a man with graying hair and a mustache, began to raise his voice a little, and Hamed did the same. "We may be getting another taxi."

I waited next to the car as Hamed and this driver went back and forth with an emotion or motive I couldn't quite identify, until it was over: haggling.

"Okay, get in. He was trying to charge us too much, it's okay now," Hamed said gesturing to me and, instantly jumping into a conversation with the driver as if they were old friends (they weren't as far as I know.) The man told Hamed that in his younger years he had worked as a driver for one of the regimes, and he pointed to places along our route where notable events occurred. I wasn't sure if any of the story was true, but Hamed seemed to take it at face value before telling the driver to pull over. To the left of the road were dusty buildings, and to the right was a seemingly empty field save for two men standing with a cart about 50 feet away.

"Hamed, what's going on? Why are we pulling over?" I asked, still reeling from our unexpected excitement at the pyramids.

"I like the carrots here. I'm getting some carrots," he said, rolling down his window and calling to one of the men. The farmer ran to the car wearing a light-colored and loosely-fitting one-piece *jalabiya*. On his head he wore a kind of turban that didn't much shield his face from a lifetime in the sun.

Hamed spoke briefly to the man before the farmer began to raise his voice a little. Hamed's reply seemed to be enough to move things along.

"What did he say, Hamed? Is there a problem?" I asked, needing a play-by-play of the scenes in Arabic progressing quickly around me.

"He was asking too much for these carrots. He knew that, and I told him I wouldn't pay that price," Hamed explained, as the farmer ran to his colleague at the cart. He grabbed an old plastic shopping bag and filled it with a variety of purple carrot that I hadn't seen before. The farmer hurried back to the car and Hamed inspected the harvest, nodding, and handing over some money.

The farmer looked at the payment, paused for a moment, and then screamed. He then began to cry, and climbed into the car window. It appeared as if the farmer was trying to hug Hamed, as the taxi driver got the hint to slowly pull away.

"Holy crap, what just happened?!" I asked, wondering what else might happen during this surreal experience.

"I gave him a little extra money for the carrots, he did a good job," Hamed said.

"How much? What was it?" I asked.

I remember Hamed telling me it was just an extra 5 Egyptian pounds, the equivalent of about $0.80 at the time. During a period in Egypt of uncertainty and a struggle for a better life, this gesture of appreciation seemed to represent the power of kindness and civility. Even a small gesture to lessen hardship seemed to hold great meaning.

Final thoughts

So much of our exploration of journalism and bread revolves around the idea of power. It's not that the practice of journalism or the subsidizing of bread are in and of themselves powerful, but they can be seen as tools to exert influence over someone or something. The famous social psychologists French and Raven categorized power into five bases: legitimate, coercive, reward, referent, and expert. A later sixth base of "informational" power created a framework to better understand the exertion of influence in different settings. A war lord threatening violence to force compliance would be exerting coercive power, for example. Voters freely electing members of their government are exerting (or granting) legitimate power. A journalist presenting discovered facts and context to inform a logical explanation of an event or subject, would perhaps demonstrate informational or even expert power.

This is not a book about power, but I present that brief oversimplication to lead us here: the more sustainable and worthwhile influence is the kind that inspires willing participation, as opposed to begrudging compliance. This may seem like a counter to Machiavelli's thoughts in the last chapter about being loved or feared, but I don't think it is. Coercing compliance is a quick and dirty tactic to see a result, while inspiring voluntary collaboration takes effort, empathy, and investment.

My visit to Cairo was during an uncertain period between regimes, in which I wasn't sure how secure I would be in the practice of journalism. I had to report myself to authorities to have some semblance of permission to conduct my interviews, which is already different than to what I'm accustomed. I hid my microphone while at different locations so as not to draw attention to myself. I hesitated to mention my nationality. Even if I wasn't expressly forbidden from a certain activity, I self-censored to a degree. It's uncomfortable.

The discourse around journalism, and more broadly about the freedom of expression and assembly, in the United States can seem insular and empty at times. American political speech is filled with hyperbole about media suppression, bias, manipulation, or malice, which may contain some truths. But it also might enter the realm of the absurd when placed alongside countries like Egypt, whether we're talking about putting bread on our tables or "bread" in our democracy. There is a lot of power at play, but inflated rhetoric doesn't always match reality.

The common link between a healthier democracy and a healthier journalism is found in the unrealized potential of an inspired citizenry. There are not enough positive actors playing the long game of effort, empathy, and investment in public education and engagement needed to build an infrastructure to withstand attempts at coercive and (dis)informational power grabs. There's been some progress in recent years to raise awareness of the pernicious effects of mis- and disinformation, but the world will need to mobilize more resources to begin purifying a tainted informational water supply.

I believe the people can ultimately wrest power from entities which would seek to dominate them, with enough time, organization, and tolerance for struggle. This requires a recognition of our shared humanity and our potential to harness our collective strength in a constructive way.

Progress may need to be made one news report, one roadside purple carrot, or one Swiss chocolate at the pyramids at a time.

Bake Bread: Egyptian Fino Bread

Egypt is a place where the word for bread "aish" literally means "life." While flatbread is a staple, fino bread is also popular. It's a smaller elongated roll, like a baguette shape without an incision to open it. Some Egyptians told me this bread was originally made by an Italian in Alexandria, but it seems to be thoroughly Egyptian.

You need:

Milk (warm): 1/2 cup
Water (warm): 1/4 cup
Butter: 1 Tbsp
Sugar: 1 Tbsp
Yeast: 2.5 tsp
Salt: 1/2 tsp
Whole wheat flour: 1 cup
Unbleached white flour/or bread flour: 1-1.5 cup
Vegetable oil: 2 Tbsp
*I've also seen recipes use an egg and a small amount of baking powder.

1) Melt butter in a pot, and add the milk, water, and sugar. Make sure the mixture isn't too hot before you add your yeast.

2) Remove the pot from heat, and add in your salt and flour. With your hand, begin to push and pull the mixture toward the side of the pot. You're essentially kneading the dough by moving it against the pot. I add in flour in waves, seeing how the consistency of the dough is feeling with the total flour being about 2 cups.

3) Begin to form the dough into a ball, in the pot. You want the dough to have enough gluten to stay together, but if it's too sticky and you're at 2 cups of flour already, add some vegetable oil instead of more flour. Cover with plastic wrap or a towel, and let it rise until doubled. This will take a while, perhaps 2 hours.

4) Once the dough is doubled, form multiple balls of dough of 70-90g each. Let those rest for about an hour.

5) Next, you'll roll out the dough with a rolling pin, before with your hands rolling it into a log. Set those logs onto a greased/oiled pan. Again, you can cover and let the dough rest another hour in a warm place.

6) Pre-heat the oven to 400F. Brush loaves with vegetable oil, butter or sugar water.

7) Bake 10-15 minutes, or until brown.

8) Enjoy with jam, butter, or dipped in your tea or coffee.

6. Get a real job

"Why don't you do something meaningful with your life?"

From anyone else this message may have seemed harsh, but as it came from a friend and former journalist, I read on with amusement and dismay.

"Why not work for a nonprofit, or work for the church, instead of staying in the news business?" I had mostly worked for nonprofit news outlets in my career, but this was clearly a call for me to consider working for a community foundation, charity, or other social service entity — something more fulfilling (or at least less "demeaning") than the dregs of reporting news.

This friend had worked in print journalism before jumping into political communications roles, and then finding a position in faith-based outreach. His somewhat random questions about my life choices didn't seem entirely out of place during the heated U.S. election season in 2016. Growing public and political scrutiny of the work and role of journalists seemed to add pressure on an already difficult profession. My friend's questions cut to an existential dilemma that many journalists have faced: Does my work in journalism amount to a higher calling, and matter as much to society as I once thought it could? And how long do I struggle to feed this industry, before needing to feed my family and my soul by doing something else?

These questions stem from an altruistic understanding of journalism that we've explored in earlier chapters of this book, seeing the profession as a vocation to help work toward the common good through good reporting, analysis, and presentation of the events of our time. It isn't just *any* job — or at least that's what we tell ourselves.

After college, I baked bread in a local food cooperative to pay for gas between news reporting jobs. After a few months of early mornings with baguettes and red pepper Asiago loaves, I was offered my first big, full-time journalism job with the NPR station in Phoenix. The catch, if it

"*Journalism is your career, and the bakery is a job. You have to move for your career.*"

could be called one, is that I would need to pack up and move within days, meaning I'd need to quit the bakery with little notice. The advice from my dad at the time was, "Journalism is your career, and the bakery is a job. You have to move for your career." He was right, and I did, but I felt guilty leaving a job I enjoyed, with people I enjoyed, on so little notice.

But I had to.

Although the craft of journalism might best be described as a trade to be learned, like baking, the identity of "journalist" can take deep root in a person's life. In 2019, researchers from the University of Kansas and La Trobe University in Australia added to a growing number of studies exploring journalist identity after leaving daily news. The study of about 350 former and current newspaper journalists in the U.S. who had lost their jobs found 47% said a career change did not affect their professional identity. Roughly 36% of those who changed careers still identify themselves as "journalists," despite being out of traditional newspaper jobs for years.

There are many factors that push a journalist to don their professional identity in a way different than they might with some trades. More than the writing, researching, and analyzing, journalists tend to observe the world in a discerning (some might say overly cynical or skeptical) way. The observation of our communities, the intent listening to nuance in political speech, the attempts at not publicly choosing sides on sticky political issues, are all activities that a journalist can't easily turn off when the work day ends, if the work day ends. Long hours of responding to news events or the availability of sources blurs the line between work and non-work, which takes a toll. If you ask a popular search engine "how many journalists are alcoholics," one of the top results might be findings from A *Study of Alcohol Use by Reporters and Editors*, a 1983 paper by a Washington State University researcher. The study presents a limited sample showing journalists were perhaps twice as likely to have serious alcohol dependence issues than the general public at the time. While I question how the results of any such study might inform our understanding of an entire industry, it's clear that heavy drinking is seen by some as part of the journalist's reality. This is perhaps related to the work of a journalist invading their sense of well-being and their sense of self, in serious and silly ways.

The albatross of duty and ambition

"Apparently a football player has been shot," my adviser told me, as I sat in the lobby of the public television station in Moscow, Idaho. In September 2004 I was the news director for the student radio station at the University of Idaho, and occasional anchor for television programs.

"Oh yeah?!" I asked, adding some flippant remark to show my disbelief. Even in college I had begun to adopt the pervasive newsroom gallows-humor, sometimes toward actual events, and other times toward fictitious scenarios.

"Someone's been shot, Mr. Ganzer. Do your job."

This was not fictitious.

Two brothers, Matthew and James Wells, had knocked on the apartment door of University of Idaho cornerback Eric McMillan. When McMillan opened the door, the pair shot him, and fled across the nearby border into Washington State. After an hours-long chase, the men were arrested to face charges including second-degree murder. A fellow student reporter and I began working the phones to gather information about the shooting, and put into practice our newly-learned court records skills.

But then came news of more deaths, this time of two men in an early-morning motorcycle crash outside a fraternity house. Neither Jason Yearout nor Jack Shannon were wearing helmets in the crash, and police said alcohol was a factor.

The deaths stunned our small university community, and gave me an unusual jolt of adrenaline in my early career as a student reporter. I produced a two-and-a-half minute radio bulletin on the events, my voice filled with nervous energy and unfamiliar responsibility.

After initially reporting the tragedy, I began to internalize the trauma. The motorcycle crashed a block from the radio station, and the shooting was within miles. While reporting the events I avoided the emotion to some degree, but then it hit me all at once. I asked the student media adviser how journalists can regularly report on horrible events and keep it all together.

"You have to partition yourself in some ways, keeping the reporting in one place and the emotional reaction somewhere else," he said, adding the stress might be what drives so many journalists to the bottle. "You manage it while you can, and then you have to stop to take care of yourself."

Recent years have seen more awareness and acceptance about mental health for journalists, especially after decades of reporters embedding themselves with troops in war zones from Kabul to Kyiv. The experience of observing, interviewing, reliving, writing, and sharing stories that sometimes approach the very worst of humanity, and sometimes the best, can seem like an affliction best managed by the journalist, but not fully avoided.

And the affliction has mutations.

Especially in our celebrity-obsessed culture, society can see journalists as public figures participating in the news and events of the day, instead of sitting apart from them. A combination of necessity and maybe vanity has elevated the personal brands of journalists to promote their work and themselves as widely as possible. For a *New York Times* reporter to appear on CNN to cross-promote important articles or reporting initiatives is a necessary part of business: any reporter would want their work amplified. This kind of promotion also benefits the reporter more directly. As journalism job cuts are a perennial concern, the journalist wants to be as visible as possible to hopefully remain employable or attractive for a book deal or life of pseudo-celebrity. It's also perhaps one reason many writers have turned to subscription newsletters on websites like Substack to build a following and generate income, independent of any one employer.

Journalists like Brian Williams, the former lead anchor for NBC Nightly News, would appear in entertainment shows like Saturday Night Live or The Tonight Show just like movie stars and musicians, cracking wise but also acting as a "voice of reason" about the news. While occasionally funny, I was always uneasy about this kind of visibility of a journalist in the world of entertainment. Why would a figure who is supposed to report and present the news need to appear on a talk show and have clips from his newscasts creatively turned into renditions of Sugar Hill Gang's "Rapper's Delight" or Snoop Dogg's "Gin and Juice?" You may think it's all in good fun, and perhaps it is, showing another side of a journalist to viewers who may have interest. Still, being a lead anchor for network news is a powerful position in its own right, and not the same as being a pure entertainer. Williams was eventually suspended for six months without pay after he acknowledged exaggerating his role in an event involving a helicopter in Iraq. By embellishing a story to gain respect or credibility, a journalist can lose all credibility in short-order. Over the years, Williams rehabilitated his career and found a new niche on the cable network MSNBC, but it's fair to say the career path was a winding road.

It is worth mentioning that part of a journalist's identity may also fuel an identity crisis. Interviewing princes and pizza magnates can prompt in some journalists a question over whether they can do more than just ask questions, and do away with the scant pay and elevated stress. Michèle Flournoy, a former Pentagon official, worked in her early career as a journalist, and told *Freakonomics Radio* of a kind of push-and-pull:

> "The honest truth is I couldn't decide which side of the interview I wanted to be on for 10 years. Even when I was working in foreign policy, I was

moonlighting for a public television station. So what forced my hand was my first job in government, which decidedly put me into the foreign policy/defense policy practitioner camp, and one side of the interview."

Self-reflection is a natural and healthy exercise, and assessing whether one's job aligns with their goals can be part of that. But assessment of whether the benefits of journalism outweigh the costs can also feed into a corrosive form of impostor syndrome. A career of interviewing, learning, and witnessing life's events to serve and inform the public has appeal, but there were moments in my career when I asked myself whether I had the ability to accomplish something myself that would be worth someone else reporting.

"Content" as it is often called now — referring to any creative product ranging from articles, to podcasts, to videos — has become ubiquitous and disposable, spurred by the democratization of technology and the broader community of stakeholders creating work that used to primarily be done by journalists. Journalism, done well, takes time, skill, and care, but how the product of that labor is received is rarely commensurate with the effort required to create it. Some of the projects in my career that garnered the most public reaction were, objectively speaking, some of the least rigorous and consequential in terms of true impact. Oftentimes people are quick to engage in superficial outrage or entertainment, but fewer will engage in deep policy discussions with broad societal implications. Think of it this way: Scores of people happily comment on and share cat videos, but fewer show the same excitement about a hard-hitting story exposing public finances. From the journalist's perspective, even if the work — cat- or non-cat related — is bolstered by a deep sense of civic duty, that will only power a journalist for so long amid death threats, online nastiness, and borderline poverty. The difficulty is compounded by the "always on" reporting lifestyle without overtime pay and with high levels of public scrutiny. This is a recipe for burnout, if not a full-scale crash-and-burn.

It's easy to see journalism as a dying profession because the numbers tell the story. Analysis from the Pew Research Center, using data from the Bureau of Labor Statistics, showed U.S. newsroom employment has fallen 26% since 2008. That year, newspaper, radio, broadcast television, cable and "other information services" recorded 114,000 employees. These employees include reporters, editors, videographers, etc. In 2020, that number was 85,000.

A separate analysis from the nonprofit Report for America using American Society of Newspaper Editors and federal data, indicated there were 55,700 newspaper reporters in 1990, down to 23,030 in 2019. The nonprofit also explained the data another way: in 1990 there were 22 newspaper journalists per 100,000 U.S. citizens. In 2019, there were just 7 per 100,000. The rise in digital publications, or nonprofit newsrooms serving small areas directly or through subsidized deployment of short-term journalists (like Report for America), does little to combat the gale force headwinds for the journalism industry.

And if society doesn't appear to value the journalism, should the journalist keep doing it?

Are you ready to come back home?

"I saw your name in a local graduates blurb from the [University of Idaho]," the e-mail began. "Priest River needs a good reporter. Are you ready to come home?"

I didn't know the woman who wrote this message, but she had clearly thought about her pitch. Her message decried the corporate consolidation of newspapers in a rural part of North Idaho, where I had spent my high school years. She complained that the reporting had devolved into rewording press releases, instead of crafting investigative reports on opioid abuse, land management, or education funding.

"We can create a local bill to purchase all of the newspapers, and employee [sic] journalists with tax money. There is no investigative local journalism going on," she concludes.

I hadn't reported from Idaho since deciding to leave my hybrid journalism and bread-baking existence for the full-time job in Phoenix nearly 15 years prior. In that time I had been a radio correspondent and host in Germany,

Switzerland, and then a drive-time public radio anchor in Ohio. While my career had taken me away from Idaho, I in fact had considered whether and under what conditions I might return. This woman who wrote the e-mail wouldn't have known that. A quick visit to an online search engine revealed this woman as a candidate for local political office, and a fairly vocal participant in local issues. Perhaps this idea to fund journalism through tax money was part of a far-fetched campaign pitch.

Far-fetched, but not unheard of.

Around the world some countries do have a broadcast license fee which is used to subsidize public broadcasting. Depending on the particular rules, a household may be billed per television, radio, or broadcast-capable internet device, imposed by inspectors who check whether or not you're tuning in to anything while living your life. The BBC has benefited from such a scheme in the UK, as have the public broadcasters in Germany and Switzerland, among others. These funding efforts do keep money flowing toward public broadcasters, and in theory do signal the importance of broadcasting to the public interest.

But broadcast license fees can also suck broadcasters into the political process in a direct way. As a correspondent for World Radio Switzerland, an English-language radio station housed within the Swiss Broadcasting Corporation, I found myself out of a job when members of the right-wing Swiss People's Party began loudly protesting why Swiss taxpayer money was funding a station broadcasting in a foreign language. Putting aside the fact about a quarter of the Swiss population at the time was foreign, and English is essential to banking, diplomacy, and pharmaceuticals (all key Swiss industries), the Swiss People's Party had a point. Switzerland has four official languages — German, French, Italian, and Romansh — and English is a tool left spoken, but not codified in law. World Radio Switzerland was eventually privatized, and as a non-EU citizen who relied on work sponsorship from the public broadcaster, I and my family had to leave.

General skepticism about the government may make such a funding scheme unlikely in the U.S., and it's difficult to imagine Americans putting up with inspectors tallying and taxing televisions. But there have already been initiatives for government support of journalism beyond the grant-making Corporation for Public Broadcasting, a private nonprofit created by Congress. As early as 2023 could see the first cohort of a California state-funded scheme to award up to 40 fellows a $50,000 stipend for at least three years to work in local newsrooms that need it. The money was to be administered by the UC Berkeley Graduate School of Journalism, built on a model used by other governments and corporate or nonprofit sources. The Google News Initiative, for example, boasts it has more than 7,000 partners, giving more than $300 million in funding for projects in more than 120 countries and territories. Funding from Google or community foundations may support pop-up journalism outfits in rural areas, pay for training or innovation, or underwrite salaries for journalists housed with other outlets.

It's about money, but it's not

While journalism does have a revenue problem, I don't think money is the primary issue. Revenue comes, in a free market, when customers believe there is value in the product worth paying for. At its core, the currency of journalism is underwritten by trust, independence, and reputation. If journalism broadly is funded only by governments or corporations, there's legitimate question whether the journalism is truly independent and sustainable, and whether the public is okay with that model. The reporters themselves may also meet outside corporate support with skepticism. For years journalism outlets have bled revenue because news aggregators — search engines, websites, social media platforms — scraped headlines and sometimes full articles to keep users in their own ecosystem, without paying full fare to the outlets which created the work. Piecemeal efforts at licensing news stories through these aggregators do little to reverse the erosion of revenue and audience suffered over decades. It's also important to note that some of the same social media companies partnering with or supporting news outlets in some way became ground zero for widespread dis- and misinformation campaigns which have infected our world, spreading rumors and breeding distrust like a lab-grown virus targeting the free press.

Part of the cost from this virus is seen in even lower levels of trust and respect for journalists, and lower levels of trust for the work produced by those journalists. As more people decry the press, fostering more distrust, the situation becomes more difficult to remedy. A Pew Research Center study in 2019 found that people who felt that news outlets valued the audience, generally had more positive views about the work the outlets were doing. For example, 36% of people who think outlets value them also felt the news outlets care about people they report on, compared to 15% of people who don't feel valued. About 46% of people who feel valued by news outlets think the outlets are highly professional, compared to just 25% of people who don't feel valued. To me, these numbers show a lack of mutual respect, or at least the perception thereof.

The more we distrust what the papers say, or the radio says, or our neighbors say, the harder it can be to strengthen our communities and tackle multifaceted and complex issues like opioid abuse, land management, or education funding. Giving the benefit of the doubt is an underrated and challenging aspect to our interactions with each other, both professionally and personally. If we begin from a place of distrust or suspicion, then everything that stems from the interaction will be influenced by that distrust. It's a contagion.

Treating the contagion of distrust requires coordinated care.

To recreate the market demand for and trust of quality journalism, there needs to be a societal effort to demystify journalism as a craft, and build news literacy into our core civic curriculum. It will take more than the occasional "current event" report in grade school to turn back the tidal wave of distrust. Instead, building local news reporting into high school requirements could spark in students and parents an understanding of what journalism looks like from the inside. Or more ambitious would be an AmeriCorps-style civic engagement program, providing grants or student loan forgiveness for hours served on community-interest journalism projects.

There are already examples of the education system being used to help fortify the future of news consumption. Finland launched a broad societal effort to combat mis- and disinformation, combining efforts of civil servants, journalists, librarians and teachers to create a program encouraging critical thought and analysis of content. "They love being detectives," one teacher told *The Guardian* of engaging students to be media skeptics. "If you also get them questioning real-life journalists and politicians about what matters to them, run mock debates and real school elections, ask them to write accurate and fake reports on them … democracy, and the threats to it, start to mean something." While teaching kids (and adults) to discern quality information from propaganda, it's important that such programs don't just fan the flames of cynicism and disinterest about journalism. It's important for society to build up positive examples of journalism's potential, instead of only fighting the most pernicious negatives.

Dis- and misinformation campaigns have infected our world, spreading rumors and breeding distrust like a lab-grown virus targeting the free press.

I've been fortunate to have lived in diverse locales like rural Idaho or the banking hub of Zurich, and those diverse experiences have helped me to learn ways to forge bonds across cultural lines, and discover unexpected new experiences. This search for cultural literacy often begins with listening, and a willingness to experience people, places, and events different than what we consider our norm. By embracing and appreciating context of a complicated world, we naturally resist isolating ourselves from different opinions, different neighbors, or different professionals. If this search beyond our selves is held as more valuable, then journalism will naturally also be seen as more valuable.

Communication, at its heart, is the exchange of ideas. It doesn't need to be an inherently destructive exercise in passing judgment, or fueling tribalism. Much of modern journalism seems to have largely lost its role outside this destruction. As such, this grand campaign to shift perception of the news media won't much matter if the industry isn't proving its potential. To many of the economic and social challenges I've touched on in this book, news outlets have responded slowly and without a long-term plan. By the time aggregators had monetized digital content, either through ad revenue or in value extracted from user data, media outlets had lost a battle. Paywalls or gated content — content requiring registration or subscription — can work if there's adequate market demand and revenue to cover costs, and that's a big *if*. Corporate or nonprofit funding of news operations or individual reporters works so long as the philanthropic impulse continues, but it's not a sustainable model because it isn't independent and scalable on its own.

The competition for audience attention is fierce, dominated by the literal and proverbial cat videos that make up content people happily ingest. News isn't always as enjoyable, while also being more expensive to produce. Some outlets combine their resources to share content, akin to a news wire service among sister publications. A consequence of this impulse to reduce cost while amplifying content for a wider audience was *churnalism*, a kind of journalistic content flow filled with shared content or wire stories in a constant stream. This shared content model, in theory, might free up reporters to focus on higher-value stories: if one outlet sends a reporter to a big event, then other outlets can send reporters to do other things. But there's no guarantee the one reporter's perspective at the event is adequate, or that some of those other reporters might not just be laid-off.

A similar risk lies in journalistic cooperatives or partnerships. While there's clear potential in sharing resources and building specialties, outlets run the risk of becoming nothing more than clearinghouses for content produced by a shrinking minority of creators. If there are fewer and fewer journalists creating content, many outlets might become shells of their old selves. In a worst case, cost reductions and partnerships leave us with groups of content distributors without many high-quality journalism creators. It's as if instead of seeing grassroots efforts to move past promising but piecemeal band-aids, there's a robust building boom of journalism Potemkin villages which are repackaging unsustainable models as compelling and new.

The sustainable answer must lie in demonstrating capability and value in journalistic products in our communities and society at-large, and inspiring the public to utilize it. The press "is like the beam of a searchlight that moves restlessly about, bringing one episode and then another out of darkness into vision. Men cannot do the work of the world by this light alone," Walter Lippmann wrote. "They cannot govern society by episodes, incidents, and eruptions. It is only when they work by a steady light of their own, that the press, when it is turned upon them, reveals a situation intelligible enough for a popular decision. The trouble lies deeper than the press, and so does the remedy."

Famed journalist Edward R. Murrow might be seen as echoing some of this sentiment more than 30 years after Lippmann's commentary. Murrow saw the potential in journalism, specifically with the growth of television broadcasting, giving a speech defending substantive programming to the Radio Television News Directors Association, that ripples forward:

> "To those who say people wouldn't look; they wouldn't be interested; they're too complacent, indifferent and insulated, I can only reply: There is, in one reporter's opinion, considerable evidence against that contention. But even if they are right, what have they got to lose? Because if they are right, and this instrument is good for nothing but to entertain, amuse and insulate, then the tube is flickering now and we will soon see that the whole struggle is lost.

> This instrument can teach, it can illuminate; yes, and even it can inspire. But it can do so only to the extent that humans are determined to use it to those ends. Otherwise, it's nothing but wires and lights in a box. There is a great and perhaps

decisive battle to be fought against ignorance, intolerance and indifference. This weapon of television could be useful."

It can only do so to the extent that humans are determined to use it to those ends.

At the end of the day, we need to support journalism that we want to see, and avoid what we don't. We should make the assessment not on our own tendency toward and recognition of bias, but on our pursuit to be better-informed citizens. It's subjective, messy, and absolutely important. But it also demands decorum to make any progress for the common good. Appeals to violence and dehumanization aren't necessary. Dialogue is necessary.

Once we begin treating the disease of distrust and disrespect through a concerted effort to re-knit the fabric of our society, I believe journalism will be reborn. Ultimately the journalism we have is simply a reflection of who we are, and what we value. If we collectively don't show that we value journalists, journalism, and a well-informed citizenry to drive democracy, then we'll continue to see journalists leave the industry, and the overall quality of the media and our democracy erode even further.

If we're not happy with what we see, maybe it's time to make a change. Talking about it openly, honestly, and respectfully is an important first step.

Let us also have the courage to take many steps beyond the first.

Bake Bread: Whole Wheat Sandwich Bread

Sandwich bread can seem very easy or deceptively difficult depending on your tastes. You want it soft, but with enough structure to complement your grilled cheeses, cold cuts, and peanut butter and jellies. There's a lot of trial-and-error in getting this bread to where you and/or your family might require, but it's worth the effort.

You need:

Water (warm): 3 cups
Sugar: 4-6 tsp
Yeast: 4 tsp (0.5 oz)
Salt: 3 tsp
Whole wheat flour: 2 cups
Unbleached white flour/or bread flour: 6 cups
Margarine: 1/4 cup

1) In a stand mixer or large bowl add your sugar and yeast, and then pour your water in, too. Let the yeast bloom for about 5 minutes.

2) I've done this process by hand, and the order of things can be followed without a stand mixer, but this recipe will describe the process with a mixer. Once the yeast have bloomed, add the 6 cups of unbleached white flour, the 2 cups of whole wheat flour, and your salt on top of the flour. You can use a spoon to begin to mix the ingredients, or I just begin my stand mixer on low. As the dough begins to form, I throw in the margarine and use a scraper to keep ingredients being integrated into the dough. Let the mixer work for about 3-5 minutes on low-medium.

3) Place your dough on a lightly-floured work surface and knead it into a nice ball. Set the dough in a greased/oiled bowl, and cover for 45 minutes to an hour, or until doubled.

4) Once the dough is doubled, on your work surface split the dough into two equal sizes. You'll need to flatten the pieces into a rough rectangle shape and roll it tightly so the shorter sides are the ends of your roll. As you roll, tuck in the ends so when you finish you have a loaf shape. This takes a little practice–don't worry if it's not perfect. Place in a greased/oiled 9 inch bread pan. Cover for about 45 minutes to an hour, or until doubled.

5) Pre-heat the oven to 375F.

6) Bake 35 minutes.

7) Let cool, understanding that the best slices come after it's had time to cool. I usually put one loaf in a plastic bag in the refrigerator, and leave the other in a bag on the counter. Enjoy!

7. Leaving daily news

I've considered this book of essays a kind of love letter to the flavor of journalism I had hoped to contribute to in a world that needs it. In one respect, love letters can provide warmth in the memory of healthy, nourishing moments of a relationship. But letters can also represent one last nostalgic bender before a relationship goes on hiatus. These essays probably amount to a mix of both.

Early in my career, just as I was leaving college, a radio program director told me to quit radio, and never look back.

"Your voice," she said, looking to the side. "It's just not...you should do something else. Radio's not for you." That kind of feedback is not an easy thing to internalize, especially hearing it before my career had gotten off the ground. I hadn't yet been tested in the crucible of daily news and become a more rounded journalist. The comment confused me more than anything, as I thought my demo tape and story samples were pretty good for someone just starting out. A confidant of mine with many years in journalism said to me an undiplomatic variation of, "the heck with her. It's one opinion and not a good one." That jolt of support motivated me to seek other opinions, mentors, and training opportunities. Was I ready to anchor a network newscast at 21 years old? No, but I was willing to begin the journey.

Journalism is an odd mix of trying to force authenticity into an unnatural setting. Reporters want sources to tell their story honestly and naturally, to be able to accurately convey the person's perspective without posturing. The reporter is also trying to be honest and authentic, especially when preparing a report for broadcast. "Be conversational," is what the voice talent consultants say. Mentors over the years encouraged me to find my own voice, and settle into my uniqueness, but it's not just about the speaking voice. I also had to try to find a balance of who I am as a person, and how I channel myself through this unnatural power dynamic of journalistic work.

When the microphones, notebooks, and cameras or phones come out, the dynamic changes for everyone involved. Some reporters seem to carry the tools of the trade as a war hammer to demonstrate their own power, versatility, and prominence in any particular interaction. "I'm the one asking questions here," their demeanor seems to say, with a hint of arrogance and disrespect. This may be why some members of the public see some journalists as arrogant and disrespectful, souring on media outlets indiscriminately. Entertainers can then more easily cloak themselves in news-like settings — comedy shows, political commentating, infomercials — to cater to an audience wanting to feel informed in some way, but ultimately being served a product playing to the beliefs of the crowd.

Journalism cosplay is a strong competitor with traditional journalism, on an industrial scale. As one example,

The Daily Show with Jon Stewart birthed a cottage industry of comedy dressed as the news, including spin-off shows from Stephen Colbert, John Oliver, Samantha Bee, Larry Wilmore, and Hasan Minhaj. These entertainers may be quick to say they are just comedians and have no tie to actual journalism. But their shows, to varying degrees, featured the trappings of news: studios dressed with big desks, like a news anchor would have; on-screen graphics, video clips, and even fully produced faux news reports with correspondents; data analysis, legal filings, and sometimes stunts to reveal a truth, as you might see from some varieties of television investigative reporters. Stephen Colbert, in his eponymous fictionalized conservative television host character, famously created his own Super PAC (political action committee) to demonstrate loopholes in the United States campaign finance system. Colbert interviewed experts, created legal entities, and shared with viewers every lesson learned. While this is a stunt done for entertainment value, it could also be seen as a kind of gonzo journalism where a reporter becomes part of the story with no claim or intention of objectivity.

Much of how an audience receives information is based on their perception of the person, network, or format delivering the material. This fact has fueled the hyper-partisan mediascape we have today, as some journalists and outlets increasingly cater to the political preferences of their core audience, while eschewing the altruistic idea of "serving the entire public." An antidote to pandering and ego-padding is humility, an underrated characteristic in journalism and in life. We often seem to do lip service to the idea of not wanting to puff our chests or inflate our egos, but it's harder in practice. Early in my career I decided that the role I wanted to play in journalism was that of a tour guide: my audience and I would be journeying together to discover something or someone in our shared world, and I wouldn't stand as an obstacle to their discovery. I'd like to think that my modicum of success in journalism validates that strategy in some way.

Humility as a catalyst

There's humility you choose to make natural and habitual, and there's humility forced upon you. This book and my decision to step away from daily news might be seen as stemming from two such moments of force.

The core ideas in many of these essays have evolved over the years, but the idea to put them in a book really solidified at the birth of my youngest child, more than three years ago. I'm a natural night owl, so I gladly stayed awake to keep the baby asleep as long as possible, giving my wife a chance at extended rest. In between episodes of baby snores and burping, I would work on this capstone project after nearly two decades in journalism. *Capstone project* implies a terminus, and in a way that's correct. A growing family requires a shift in mindset, and a shift in family resources. For me, this meant looking at both the tangible and intangible realities of life as a radio host to decide whether I was happy with the conditions, prospects, and effects of the lifestyle. Is my family in the best spot I can provide for them? Am I in an environment encouraging me to be the best person I can be? As my wife and I have been blessed with a fairly large family, this kind of existential reflection has become part of my everyday.

A growing family requires a shift in mindset, and a shift in family resources.

Then, in March 2020, as the United States began seeing the first whitecaps of the COVID-19 waves to come, I was hit by a car. A driver made an illegal U-turn and took my motor scooter from under me, leaving me with a fractured wrist, separated shoulder, and a kind of PTSD anytime I rode through intersections. In an instant, I couldn't use my hands to continue typing out this book, make bread, or, more importantly, pick up my baby and fulfill the duties of husband, father, and person as I was accustomed. I thankfully have a wife and family that supported me as I tried to figure out how to adapt in humility.

It's too easy to say I left daily news because of the crash, or because of COVID-19, or the birth of my child. Though I'm religious and quite aware of the inevitability of death, it's true that having a confrontation with my mortality at the hood of an oncoming car accelerated my timeline for realigning some things in my life. But to a degree, I've always wondered whether the newsroom was the best place for me, my interests, and my goals for myself and my family. I once asked a former journalist-turned-diplomat whether it was difficult to leave the news behind and he said, "It's easier than you think."

I didn't fully understand this until taking a big-picture view of myself. Ultimately it seemed that the many compromises I had made over the years to try to fit my goals into the boxes of opportunity that the news business was presenting had led me too far from where I needed to be for personal and professional growth, health, and development.

Whereas earlier in my life I had to leave bread baking for journalism, I now was leaving journalism for new adventures and, after healing from the crash, my hobby bread baking was a companion on both sides of the decision.

Icarus and insight

I've long held a desire to test myself and chart a path beyond anyone's expectations, chiefly my own. Since the age of about 17 an internal clarion call has warned me that time is running short.

I have to learn more.

Do more.

Live more.

With that impulse came a realization that the drive to grow and exceed expectations may not be in other people's best interest, but you should still persevere. In some young people a lust for "more" can provoke recklessness, but in me it provoked my best effort at excellence. Seeking perfection is a fool's errand, but to reach for excellence by doing the best you can, well, that seemed more realistic.

I'm not sure whether this inner alarm is a personal tick, or some offshoot of my faith, but it drives me forward with a nudge to go a little farther in search of improvement; to try one more time with a little more effort.

Crises tend to knock our priorities and senses into realignment.

Early in my career, my challenges — as anyone's — were multi-fold; personal and professional, and I couldn't even recognize all of them until much later. For the sake of discretion I won't explore everything in a public memoir, but I'll say I faced a string of events which made me feel that my value as a person and as a journalist were questioned. There were moments when I had to stand on what I understood as right, honorable, and just in the practice of journalism and beyond it, and risk my livelihood standing by my core beliefs. I've coped with depression in my life. I've coped with bullies in my life. I have had to slay demons that tempt me to be complacent and stale. It's in this context that I have also worked hard to seek ways to create positive momentum to escape negative environments.

In the Greek myth of Icarus, we know he flew too high to the sun and melted his wings. It's a powerful story: don't be too prideful, or boastful, or self-confident — you'll crash back down. Those are useful guidelines, but as author Seth Godin points out, this shorthand ignores the story's other important point: Icarus was also warned not to fly too low. If Icarus flew too low — became complacent — he would face the dampness of the sea, also causing him to crash.

I always think of Icarus when listening to a favorite hip-hop track: "You Know Who You Are" by Oddisee.

"*Man can only go so high before he reaches where he can't breathe,*" he says, noting at the top of the competitive mountain, the air is thin. Some people can't walk the difficult road toward the top, and some people leave their dreams as dreams.

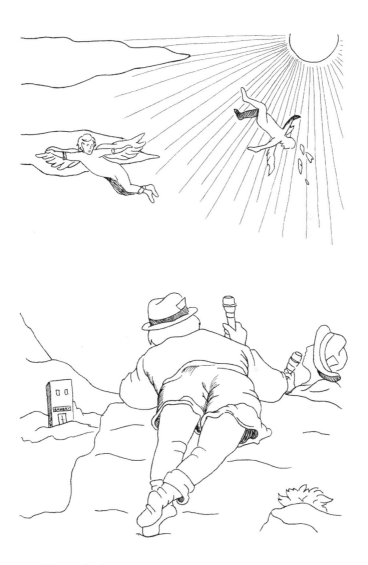

Expand the realm between Icarus' sun and sea.

"*Let them sleep on their dreams, you stay lying awake, you stay eyeing the cake,*" he says. People may try to convince you that your ambition is actually a dysfunction, and you could settle for "less than." They may lie to or about you, and try to get in your head. You have to be willing to bet on yourself when others won't or can't.

Completing an MBA program was part of the investment in myself, undertaken with a specific purpose: expand the realm between Icarus' sun and sea in which I can be a better communicator, learner, and person. If the current state of journalism was giving me boxes too small for my full self to fit into, then I needed to find other boxes.

Oddisee uses the title of the song to reinforce lessons learned from different characters in his journey. To the ones who helped him, he doesn't even need to say their name because they know. The naysayers equally don't get a specific mention, because "you know who you are," without him saying it. He finishes the song by telling us to let those naysayers see us prevail: I like to think it means in terms of prevailing in self-improvement and growth. All along the path of development, aspiration, and the associated hardships, you must be sure never to forget that "you know who you are," even when others may not see or recognize your vision.

This final point is an important one, especially when efforts toward positive growth and momentum run head-long into paradigms that refuse to be shifted. As you're knocked down, remember who you are, what your priorities are, and what you've accomplished and learned to become who you are today. For now, I'm continuing this, my next phase outside of the newsroom, with a hope that journalism's evolution will better fulfill its potential for enriching our democracy, instead of being used to feed the worst reactionary and divisive impulses of a weary public.

I'm not discounting the possibility that I might one day return to a newsroom, but I'm also not yet eager to return. My journalism and bread baking skills will be used in different settings for a while, still supporting my vocation in ways I probably haven't imagined.

Acknowledgements

This collection of essays doesn't represent the whole of my thoughts and experiences related to journalism, but I hope it contributes in a positive way to the conversation about the news business and society, and honors the many people who have helped me become who I am today. I'm incredibly thankful to all whose direct and indirect support of this project helped it to become a reality, with some of them named here.

First, I thank my wife, Katie, whose own curiosity, urging, encouragement, and loving support have inspired and aided me in my quest to be a better person and journalist. She gracefully put up with my many random German grammar questions as we prepared for life abroad, just as she experienced with me over the years random news reporting trips ranging from a moonbeam collector in the Arizona desert, to covering asylum policy on the Swiss-Italian border. Katie also encouraged this project to be much more comprehensive than I first envisioned. Her discerning eye, thoughtful critique, and patience with my many tangents about bread and journalism kept the foundation of this work strong, just as she keeps our family strong. For this and many reasons unsaid here, thank you for the honor of learning from you, dreaming with you, and sharing this life together. I love you.

To my parents, thank you for your loving encouragement to explore, and asking only that I try my best in whatever

I do. From the road to Eagle Scout to reporting in Cairo, you have been supportive, honest, and willing to learn about the world along with me. For this project especially, I thank my mom, Diane, for her advocacy for me to be creative and remember my worth. Thank you for your strength and effort to keep our family focused on what's most important.

Thank you to the many instructors and professors at the University of Idaho who gave me a tremendous foundation in journalism, writing, and communications. Thank you Glenn Mosley for showing me that public radio was an option for a young journalist, and for giving me opportunities to explore my potential. Thank you Kenton Bird for helping to build the journalism program as one of integrity, skill, and also good humor. To Brian Beesley, who edited these essays, thank you for our continued conversations about all things journalism and life, and for not bleeding too much red ink on the drafts. Thank you also to Dave Cuiller for bringing together so many of us in the masterpiece journalism training video "The Jayson Blair Witch Project." I'd like to thank Shawn O'Neal, Jeff Kimberling, Andrea Schiers, and also my memoir instructor, acclaimed author Kim Barnes, for introducing me to creative non-fiction in a supportive way.

To my journalism colleagues through the years, thank you for collaborating, learning, and fighting the good fight with me. I am thankful to Tom Banse for letting me fill in for him at the Olympia Bureau of N3, and try on this profession for real, and to Austin Jenkins for allowing me to learn from him. Thank you Cathy Duchamp for being a great editor, and for encouraging me to find my voice. Thank you to the Arizona dream team of Steve Goldstein, Paul Atkinson, and Mark Brodie for your friendship, counsel, and expertise during a fascinating time. Thank you also to Chris Furphy for your advice on wearing motorcycle helmets, and to Bill Shedd for giving me extra shifts to become a better broadcaster. Thank you Troy Pottgen and Robrt Pela for trusting me to help with sound design and bringing your creative commentaries to listeners, and also for being great friends. Thanks Louis Stanley for believing in me to develop the teen radio project pilot in Phoenix, which became a refuge for me, and that eventually blossomed into something much bigger. I thank Ros Atkins for being a kind and genuine person to me as I was a young producer, and for being a friend and inspiration to me as I was a slightly older journalist. Thank you to Marketplace correspondent Stephen Beard and Frontline's Michael Kirk for graciously giving practical advice and encouragement. Thanks Kyle James, Teri Schultz, Katharina Bart, and Andrew Curry for the real talk about being a foreign correspondent, and great encouragement. I express gratitude also to Dierk Seeburg for helping to unlock German language and culture for me. Thank you to my Poynter training cohort, especially Brian Bull and Jennifer Szweda Jordan. Brian, you are a great journalist and friend, and I thank you for your support and inspiration through victories and setbacks. Jennifer, thank you for your example applying your faith and values in your work and life, and for being such a good friend to our family.

To Philippe Mottaz, thank you for believing in me and the kind of journalism I wanted to do. I learned a lot from you and your vision of Swiss media. Thank you to the Zurich bureau chief Vincent Landon for your friendship and candor, especially during those long days reporting in Davos. Thank you also to Fred Blassel for your continued support and wisdom in journalism and out of journalism. Thank you Lucas Chambers, Fabrice Junod, Jordan Davis, David Glaser, Mirko Toppano, and so many others for the great conversations during the heyday of World Radio Switzerland.

Thank you David Molpus for giving me the opportunity to build a drive-time shift as I envisioned, and for being a candid and trusted resource and friend. Thank you also Dave Kanzeg for encouraging calculated risks in programming, and embracing an international perspective. Thanks Barbara Whitlow for being such a great teammate to lead success in afternoon radio, for sharing with me a desire to escape parochial thinking, and for valuable feedback on the early versions of these essays. To Maxie C. Jackson III, thank you for being real and for empowering your team to build things and not just tear things down. Mike McIntyre thank you for your friendship and perspective during challenging times. Thanks Gabriel Kramer for being a kind and skilled producer during one of my most difficult moments, and for your continued friendship. Thank you Michelle Faust Raghavan, Liz Miller, and Darrielle Snipes for your friendship and for keeping it real; David C. Barnett, Nick Castele, Glenn Forbes, Dan Polletta, Sarah Jane Tribble, and Drew Maziasz for great conversation during and not during live radio; Jeff Carlton, Al Dahlhausen, and John DeBarr, for being trusted colleagues and friends.

I want to thank Sean Watterson for creating a space for a modern-day salon that brought global affairs into the community, and encouraging positive civic involvement and collaboration. Thank you Josh Stacher and Pete Moore for your friendship, authenticity and passion, and for always making me feel like our contributions in the public square mattered (they do!) Thank you Stephanie Jansky, Dan Moulthrop, Heather Hodges, Carina Van Vliet, Milena Sterio, Michael Scharf, Teddy Eisenberg, and all who helped cultivate in Cleveland a vibrant international affairs ecosystem.

I want to express gratitude to the Arthur F. Burns Fellowship program, and the inimitable Frank Dieter-Freiling, and to the legacy of the Robert Bosch Foundation Fellowship and so many of its alumni who are friends. Thank you Achim Wendler for your wisdom in Munich and Berlin, and to other "Burnsies" including Jan Hendrik Becker, Georg Kern, Fabian Löhe, Susanne Amann, and all of my colleagues at German media outlets who let me learn from them including Walter Kittel and Diego Vanzi. Thank you to Sultan Sooud Al-Qassemi for your promotion of cultural literacy and exchange, and your work to bring real-time information from the "Arab Uprisings" to English-speakers. Thank you also for being so gracious and kind with your time and perspective in Zurich.

A special thank you also to my friend David Patrician for helping me understand the German media world, and for all of the real talk about family, friendships, and the expat life.

My thanks is also extended to the many friends and family members not specifically mentioned here, but whose influence in my life certainly contributed to my practice of journalism. Also, my gratitude to the scores of people who trusted me to help tell their stories in reports over the years, and to the audience for joining me on the exploration of our world (and bread.)

Lastly, thank you in advance to my children for all of the things you will do in your life, big and small, to try to make things a little better than you found them. You've already inspired so much within me, and I look forward to seeing how you explore, travel, communicate, dream, and build connections.

Bibliography

The Gallows and the Kitchen Table:

Anderson, Jane, and Den Trumbull. "The Benefits of the Family Table." *American College of Pediatricians.* May 2014, www.acpeds.org/the-college-speaks/position-statements/parenting-issues/the-benefits-of-the-family-table. Accessed 17 March 2019.

Halpin, Tony. "Plans for education reform get a cool reception from parents." *The Sunday Times.* 26 October 2005, www.thetimes.co.uk/article/plans-for-education-reform-get-a-cool-reception-from-parents-2hzs0vmgxlk. Accessed 15 March 2019.

Leeper, Thomas J. "No Politics at the Dinner Table?" *Psychology Today.* 22 November 2012, www.psychologytoday.com/us/blog/polarized/201211/no-politics-the-dinner-table. Accessed 15 March 2019.

Murrow, Edward R. RTDNA Convention, 15 October 1958. rtdna.org/content/edward_r_murrow_s_1958_wires_lights_in_a_box_speech. Accessed 13 April 2019.

Perrigo, Billy. "'Rope. Tree. Journalist. Some Assembly Required': Walmart Removes Threatening Shirt From Store." *Time.* 1 December 2017, time.com/5044596/rope-tree-journalist-walmart-shirt-removed-threatening. Accessed 17 March 2019.

"Walmart pulls threatening shirt at RTDNA's urging." RTDNA. 30 November 2017, www.rtdna.org/article/walmart_pulls_threatening_shirt_at_rtdna_s_urging. Accessed 8 October 2022.

Zadrozny, Brandy. "The Man Behind 'Journalist, Rope, Tree.'" *The Daily Beast*. 8 November 2016. www.thedailybeast.com/the-man-behind-journalist-rope-tree. Accessed 13 April 2019.

Zengerle, Patricia and Richard Cowan. "'Mike Pence deserves it': Trump's ire at VP a focus of U.S. Capitol riot hearings." *Reuters*. 10 June 2022, www.reuters.com/world/us/mike-pence-deserves-it-trumps-ire-vp-focus-us-capitol-riot-hearings-2022-06-10. Accessed 12 June 2022.

1: Defining Journalism with a Bread Rebellion

Auerbach, Stephen. "Politics, Protest, and Violence in Revolutionary Bourdeaux: 1789-1794." *Journal of Western French History*, vol. 37, pp. 149-161.

Bourne, Henry E. "Food Control and Price Fixing in Revolutionary France: I." *The Journal of Political Economy*, vol. 27, no. 2, 1919, pp. 73-94.

Bouton, Cynthia A. "Gendered Behavior in Substinence Riots: The French Flour War of 1775." *Journal of Social History*, vol. 23, no. 4, 1990, pp. 735-754.

Bramen, Lisa. "When Food Changed History: The French Revolution." *Smithosonian Magazine*, 14 July 2010. www.smithsonianmag.com/arts-culture/when-food-changed-history-the-french-revolution-93598442. Accessed 8 Oct 2022.

Chisick, Harvey. "Pamphlets and Journalism in the Early French Revolution: The offices of the Ami du Roi of the Abbé Royou as a Center of Royalist Propaganda." *French Historical Studies*, vol. 15, no. 4, 1988, pp. 623-645.

Ellison, Sarah. "A veteran newspaper editor grapples with a seemingly simple question: What is journalism?" *The Washington Post*, 21 December 2018. www.washingtonpost.com/entertainment/books/a-veteran-newspaper-editor-grapples-with-a-seemingly-simple-question-what-is-journalism/2018/12/20/505de5e2-03d2-11e9-b6a9-0aa5c2fcc9e4_story.html. Accessed 29 May 2019.

"Journalism." *Merriam-Webster Dictionary*, May 21, 2019, Merriam-Webster. www.merriam-webster.com/dictionary/journalism. Accessed 29 May 2019.

Kaplan, Steven Laurence. "The Paris Bread Riot of 1725." *French Historical Studies*, vol. 14, no. 1, 1985, pp. 23-56.

Kovach, Bill and Tom Rosenstiel. *The Elements of Journalism* (3rd ed.) Crown, 2014.

Kurtz, Howard. "Media's failure on Iraq still stings." CNN, 11 March 2013. www.cnn.com/2013/03/11/opinion/kurtz-iraq-media-failure/index.html. Accessed 8 Oct 2022.

Lippmann, Walter. *Public Opinion*. Harcourt, Brace and Company, 1922.

Luebering, J.E. "Philip Freneau." *Encyclopedia Brittanica*, 28 January 2016. www.britannica.com/biography/Philip-Freneau#ref1229696. Accessed 29 May 2019.

Popkin, Jeremy D. "The Provincial Newspaper Press and Revolutionary Politics." *French Historical Studies*, vol. 18, no. 2, 1993, pp. 434-456.

Todd, Tony. "French revolutionary rule keeps Paris bakers baking." *France 24*, 15 Aug 2013. www.france24.com/en/20130815-french-revolutionary-rule-keeps-bakers-paris. Accessed 8 Oct 2022.

"What is journalism?" Journalism Essentials, *American Press Institute*, www.americanpressinstitute.org/journalism-essentials/what-is-journalism. Accessed 29 May 2019.

"What makes journalism different than other forms of communication?" Journalism Essentials, *American Press Institute*, www.americanpressinstitute.org/journalism-essentials/what-is-journalism/makes-journalism-different-forms-communication. Accessed 29 May 2019.

"U.S. Diplomacy and Yellow Journalism, 1895–1898." *Milestones in the History of U.S. Foreign Relations*, Department of State Office of the Historian. history.state.gov/milestones/1866-1898/yellow-journalism. Accessed 11 Oct 2022.

2: Why Journalism Education Can Help Us All

"27-3022 Reporters and Correspondents." *Occupational Employ-ment Statistics.* Bureau of Labor Statistics, May 2018, www.bls.gov/oes/current/oes273022.htm. Accessed 15 Aug 2019.

Beaujon, Andrew. "This week's 4 arguments against j-school." *The Poynter Institute,* 21 Sept. 2012, www.poynter.org/report-ing-editing/2012/this-weeks-4-arguments-against-j-school/. Accessed 15 Aug. 2019.

Camp, Michael. "The J-School Debate: Is the Timing Finally Right for University Journalism Programs and the Rest of the University Community to Work Together?" *The Journal of General Education,* vol. 61, no. 3, pp. 240-263.

"Cost of Attendance." *Columbia Journalism School,* journal-ism.columbia.edu/cost-attendance. Accessed 15 Aug. 2019.

Deutsches Brotinstitut e.V. www.brotinstitut.de. Accessed 15 Aug. 2019.

Ganzer, Tony. "In Defense of Journalism Education." *Anthony-Ganzer.com,* 20 Oct 2012. www.anthonyganzer.com/dis-patches/media-studies/ in-defense-of-journalism-education. Accessed 5 Nov 2022.

King, Susan. "The Carnegie-Knight Initiative on the Future of Journalism Education: improving how journalists are educated & how their audiences are informed." *Daedalus*, vol. 139, no. 2, pp. 126-137.

Loxton, Rachel. "Germany wastes 1.7 million tons of bread a year." *The Local*, 5 Oct. 2018, www.thelocal.de/20181005/germany-wastes-17-million-tons-of-bread-a-year. Accessed 15 Aug. 2019.

O'Brien, Meredith. "Teaching Journalism in the Age of Trump." *Inside Higher Ed*, 10 May 2019. www.insidehighered.com/advice/2019/05/10/journalism-professor-describes-challenges-teaching-students-trump-era-opinion. Accessed 8 Oct 2022.

Pulitzer, Joseph. "The College of Journalism." *The North American Review*, vol. 178 no. 570, May 1904, pp. 641-680.

Schramm, Wilbur L. "Education for Journalism: Vocational, General, or Professional?" *The Journal of General Education*, vol. 1, no. 2, January 1947, pp. 90-98.

"Unser täglich Brot." WWF, 4 Oct. 2018, www.wwf.de/2018/oktober/unser-taeglich-brot/. Accessed 15 Aug. 2019.

"Update 1-Germany's 2018 wheat and rapeseed crops seen down." *Reuters*, 16 May 2018, www.reuters.com/article/grains-germany/update-1-germanys-2018-wheat-and-rapeseed-crops-seen-down-idUSL5N1SN50Z. Accessed 15 Aug. 2019.

Yun, Hyun Jung. "Wilbur Schramm." *Encyclopedia Britannica*, 1 Aug. 2022, www.britannica.com/biography/Wilbur-Schramm. Accessed 8 October 2022.

3: Journalists Not 'Journalists'

Associated Press. "Court: Bloggers have First Amendment protections." USA *Today*, 20 Jan 2014. www.usatoday.com/story/tech/2014/01/20/defamation-bloggers-supreme-court/4658295. Accessed 8 Oct 2022.

"Ausbildung zum Bäcker/in." *Ausbildung.de.* www.ausbildung.de/berufe/baecker. Accessed 8 Oct 2022.

Dienst, Alexandra. "Leider gilt die Devise, Geiz ist geil." *Deutschlandfunk*, 24 April 2019. www.deutschlandfunk.de/baeckereien-leider-gilt-die-devise-geiz-ist-geil-100.html. Accessed 8 Oct 2022.

Dzur, Albert W. "Public Journalism and Deliberative Democracy." *Polity*, vol. 34, no. 3, Spring 2022, pp. 313-336.

Ganzer, Tony. "'Journalistic Outsourcing:' Not the journalism I grew up with." *AnthonyGanzer.com*, 9 Feb 2013. www.anthonyganzer.com/dispatches/media-studies/not-the-journalism-i-grew-up-with. Accessed 5 Nov 2022.

Harkin, James. "Journalism is now the second draft of history." *Columbia Journalism Review*, 14 Jan 2019. www.cjr.org/opinion/journalism-is-now-the-second-draft-of-history.php. Accessed 8 Oct 2022.

Hodgetts, Darrin, Kerry Chamberlain, Margaret Scammell, Rolinda Karapu and Linda Waimarie Nikora. "Constructing health news: possibilities for a civic-oriented journalism." *Health*, vol. 12, no. 1, January 2008, pp. 43-66.

Ich mach's. 2020. "Unser Täglich Brot." *Bayerischer Rundfunk video.* 7 Sept. www.br.de/fernsehen/ard-alpha/sendungen/ich-machs/im-baecker100.html.

"Journalist/in Ausbildung Gehalt." *Ausbildung.de.* www.ausbildung.de/berufe/journalist/gehalt. Accessed 8 Oct 2022.

Kelly, Tadhg. "What Is Journalism Anymore?" *TechCrunch*, 9 Nov 2014. techcrunch.com/2014/11/09/what-is-journalism-anymore. Accessed 8 Oct 2022.

Kirchner, Lauren. "Bloggers versus the courts." *Columbia Journalism Review*, 29 Jan 2014. archives.cjr.org/behind_the_news/sued_bloggers_state-level_free.php. Accessed 8 Oct 2022.

Lepore, Jill. "Does Journalism Have a Future?" *The New Yorker*, 21 Jan 2021. www.newyorker.com/magazine/2019/01/28/does-journalism-have-a-future. Accessed 8 Oct 2022.

"New Zealand's highest court: Anyone can be a journalist, and that includes bloggers." *GigaOm*, 18 Sept 2014. old.gigaom.com/2014/09/18/new-zealands-highest-court-joins-growing-consensus-anyone-can-be-a-journalist-and-that-includes-bloggers. Accessed 8 Oct 2022.

White, Aidan. "Ethics 101: What is Journalism and Who is a Journalist?" *Ethical Journalism Network*, 17 Feb 2015. ethicaljournalismnetwork.org/what-is-journalism-who-is-journalist. Accessed 8 Oct 2022.

"What is journalism for?" *Columbia Journalism Review*, Sept/Oct 2013. archives.cjr.org/cover_story/what_is_journalism_for.php. Accessed 8 Oct 2022.

4: Media, Machiavelli, and Power

Benner, Erica. "Have we got Machiavelli all wrong?" *The Guardian*, 3 March 2017. www.theguardian.com/books/2017/mar/03/have-we-got-machiavelli-all-wrong. Accessed 8 Oct 2022.

Brown, Shelby. "Baking Bread the Roman Way." *Getty*, 29 May 2020. www.getty.edu/news/baking-bread-the-roman-way. Accessed 8 Oct 2022.

Chiappini, Luciano. "House of Este." *Encyclopedia Brittanica*. www.britannica.com/topic/House-of-Este. Accessed 8 Oct 2022.

Davis, William P. "'Enemy of the People': Trump Breaks Out This Phrase During Moments of Peak Criticism." *The New York Times*, 19 July 2018. www.nytimes.com/2018/07/19/business/media/trump-media-enemy-of-the-people.html. Accessed 8 Oct 22.

Farhi, Paul. "Anonymous sources are increasing in news stories, along with rather curious explanations." *The Washington Post*, 15 Dec 2013. /www.washingtonpost.com/lifestyle/style/anonymous-sources-are-increasing-in-news-stories-along-with-rather-curious-explanations/2013/12/15/5049a11e-61ec-11e3-94ad-004fefa61ee6_story.html. Accessed 5 Nov 2022.

Farrell, Michael. "Anonymous Sources." *Society of Professional Journalists*. www.spj.org/ethics-papers-anonymity.asp. Accessed 5 Nov 2022.

"Follow the Money." *Slate*, 5 Nov 1998. slate.com/news-and-politics/1998/11/follow-the-money.html. Accessed 5 Nov 2022.

Ganzer, Tony. "Journalists should stop subsidizing the pundit class." *AnthonyGanzer.com*, 21 Sept 2019. www.anthonyganzer.com/dispatches/media-studies/journalists-should-stop-subsidizing-the-pundit-class. Accessed 5 Nov 2022.

Ganzer, Tony. "The scourge of 'anonymous sources.'" *AnthonyGanzer.com*, 24 Feb 2019. www.anthonyganzer.com/dispatches/media-studies/the-scourge-of-anonymous-sources. Accessed 5 Nov 2022.

Hughes, Rebecca Ann. "The Italian Town Where You Can Eat Like a Renaissance Royal." *Atlas Obscura*, 22 Feb 2022. www.atlasobscura.com/articles/ferrara-italy-renaissance-food. Accessed 8 Oct 2022.

Keneally, Meghan. "Donald Trump calls media 'the enemy of the American People.'" ABC *News*, 17 Feb 2017. abcnews.go.com/Politics/donald-trump-calls-media-enemy-american-people/story?id=45572928. Accessed 8 Oct 22.

Machiavelli, Niccolò. *The Prince*. 1532.

Merrill, John Calhoun. *The Princely Press: Machiavelli On American Journalism*. Lanham, MD: University Press of America, 1998.

Messisbugo, Cristoforo di. *Banchetti composizione di vivande e apparecchio generale*. 1549. www.google.com/books/edi-

tion/Banchetti_compositioni_di_vivande_et_app/
9yA8AAAAcAAJ. Accessed 8 Oct 2022.

Monaco, Farrell. "Baking Bread with the Romans: Part III – The
Panis Quadratus Strikes Back." *Tavola Mediterranea*, 14 June
2018. tavolamediterranea.com/2018/06/14/baking-bread-
romans-part-iii-panis-strikes-back. Accessed 8 Oct 2022.

Oremus, Will. "Why journalists should stop asking President
Trump multipart questions." *Slate*, 21 March 2017. slate.com/
news-and-politics/2017/03/why-journalists-should-
never-ask-donald-trump-multipart-questions.html.
Accessed 8 Oct 2022.

Stelter, Brian and Bill Carter. "For Instant Ratings, Interviews
With a Checkbook." *The New York Times*, 12 June 2011.
www.nytimes.com/2011/06/13/business/media/13pay-
ments.html. Accessed 5 Nov 2022.

Tapper, Jake and Jeremy Herb. "Author of 2018 'Anonymous' op-
ed critical of Trump revealed." CNN, 28 Oct 2020.
www.cnn.com/2020/10/28/politics/anonymous-new-
york-times-oped-writer. Accessed 5 Nov 2022.

Taylor, Miles. "I Am Part of the Resistance Inside the Trump
Administration." *The New York Times*, 5 Sept 2018.
www.nytimes.com/2018/09/05/opinion/trump-white-
house-anonymous-resistance.html. Accessed 5 Nov 2022.

Tugend, Alina. "Pundits for Hire." *American Journalism Review*,
May 2003. ajrarchive.org/article.asp?id=2995&id=2995.
Accessed 5 Nov 2022.

"Where is Asiago made?" *Asiago Formaggio DOP*. asiagocheese.it/en/origin. Accessed 8 Oct 2022.

5: Bread Diplomacy and Egyptian Revolution

Ali, Sadaf R. and Shahira Fahmy. "Gatekeeping and citizen journalism: The use of social media during the recent uprisings in Iran, Egypt, and Libya." *Media, War & Conflict*, vol. 6, no. 1, April 2013, pp. 55-69.

Bess, Michael. "E.P. Thompson." *Encyclopedia Brittanica*. www.britannica.com/biography/E-P-Thompson. Accessed 8 Oct 2022.

Black, Ian. "Struggling country where bread means life." *The Guardian*, 11 April 2008. www.theguardian.com/world/2008/apr/12/egypt.food. Accessed 8 Oct 2022.

Blue, Richard N. and David W. Dunlop, Michael Goldman, and Lloyd S. Harbert. "PL 480 Title I: The Egyptian Case." *U.S. Agency for International Development*, June 1983. pdf.usaid.gov/pdf_docs/Pnaal015.pdf. Accessed 8 Oct 2022.

Dethier, Jean-Jacques and Kathy Funk. "The Language of Food: PL 480 in Egypt." *MERIP Middle East Report*, no. 145, The Struggle for Food, March-April 1987, pp. 22-28.

Durisin, Megan. "Egypt Wheat Imports May Fall to 9-Year Low as War Disrupts Trade." *Bloomberg*, 29 March 2022. www.bloomberg.com/news/articles/2022-03-29/egypt-wheat-imports-may-fall-to-9-year-low-as-war-disrupts-trade. Accessed 8 Oct 2022.

"Egyptian Demonstrations Hit Sadat's Political, Economic Policies." *MERIP Reports*, no. 34, January 1975, pp. 28-29.

"Egyptian satirist Bassem Youssef stops show, fearing for safety." *Deutsche Welle*, 3 June 2014. www.dw.com/en/egyptian-satirist-bassem-youssef-stops-show-fearing-for-safety/a-17678157. Accessed 8 Oct 22.

El Safty, Sarah. "Egypt's wheat imports from Russia rose in March despite war." *Reuters*, 5 April 2022. www.reuters.com/world/middle-east/egypts-wheat-imports-russia-rose-march-despite-war-2022-04-05. Accessed 8 Oct 2022.

Ganzer, Tony. "Part 1: 'We don't know who is manipulating whom.'" *World Radio Switzerland*, 25 Mar 2012. www.anthonyganzer.com/radio-samples/interviews/part-1-we-dont-know-who-is-manipulating-whom. Accessed 8 Oct 2022.

Ganzer, Tony. "Part II: Back home again in revolutionary Cairo." *World Radio Switzerland*, 25 Mar 2012. www.anthonyganzer.com/radio-samples/egypt/back-home-again-in-revolutionary-cairo. Accessed 8 Oct 2022.

Ganzer, Tony. "Part 4: A walk through Cairo's revolutionary streets." *World Radio Switzerland*, 25 Mar 2012. www.anthonyganzer.com/radio-samples/egypt/part-4-a-walk-through-cairos-revolutionary-streets. Accessed 8 Oct 2022.

Jailani, Yusuf. "Breadbaskets and Breakdowns: Food Shocks and Political Instability in the Arab World." *Harvard International Review*, vol. 37, no. 3, Spring 2016, pp. 52-54.

Kandil, Amr Mohamed. "How Muslim Brotherhood lost people's trust in 2 years." *Egypt Today*, 13 July 2018. www.egypt-today.com/Article/1/53906/How-Muslim-Brotherhood-lost-people%E2%80%99s-trust-in-2-years. Accessed 8 Oct 22.

Makollus, Stefan and Martina Mollenhauer. "Technical Profile: Bread is 'life' in Egypt." *World Grain*, 24 Oct 2017. www.world-grain.com/articles/8765-technical-profile-bread-is-life-in-egypt. Accessed 8 Oct 2022.

Marfleet, Philip. "Mubarak's Egypt—Nexus of Criminality." *State Crime Journal*, vol. 2, no. 2, Autumn 2013, pp. 112-134.

Murphy, Dan. "Bread riots or bankruptcy: Egypt faces stark economic choices." *Christian Science Monitor*, 3 April 2013. www.csmonitor.com/World/Middle-East/2013/0403/Bread-riots-or-bankruptcy-Egypt-faces-stark-economic-choices. Accessed 8 Oct 2022.

Northouse, Peter G. *Leadership: Theory and Practice*. 8th ed., Sage, 2019.

Parfitt, Tom. "Vladimir Putin bans grain exports as drought and wildfires ravage crops." *The Guardian*, 5 Aug 2010. www.theguardian.com/world/2010/aug/05/vladimir-putin-ban-grain-exports. Accessed 8 Oct 2022.

Sadiki, Larbi. "Towards Arab Liberal Governance: From the Democracy of Bread to the Democracy of the Vote." *Third World Quarterly*, vol 18, no. 1, March 1997, pp. 127-148.

Shoshan, Boaz. "Grain Riots and the "Moral Economy": Cairo, 1350-1517." *The Journal of Interdisciplinary History*, vol. 10, no. 3, Winter 1980, pp. 459-478.

Slackman, Michael. "Bread, the (subsidized) stuff of life in Egypt." *The New York Times*, 16 Jan 2008. www.nytimes.com/2008/ 01/16/world/africa/16iht-bread.4.9271958.html. Accessed 8 Oct 2022.

Stacher, Joshua. *Watermelon Democracy: Egypt's Turbulent Transition*. United States: Syracuse University Press, 2020.

Thompson, E.P. "The Moral Economy of the English Crowd in the Eighteenth Century." *Past & Present*, no. 50, February 1971, pp. 76-136.

Trego, Rachel. "The functioning of the Egyptian food-subsidy system during food-price shocks." *Development in Practice*, vol. 21, no. 4/5, June 2011, pp. 666-678.

"World Bank Group to Extend Current Strategy in Egypt to Maintain Momentum on Reforms." *The World Bank*, 30 April 2019. www.worldbank.org/en/news/press-release/2019/ 04/30/world-bank-group-to-extend-current-strategy-in-egypt-to-maintain-momentum-on-reforms. Accessed 8 Oct 2022.

6: Get a Real Job

Cooper, Gael Fashingbauer. "Brian Williams raps 'Gin and Juice' with Jimmy Fallon's help." *Today*, 22 April 2014. www.today.com/popculture/brian-williams-raps-gin-juice-jimmy-fallons-help-1D79560418. Accessed 8 Oct 2022.

Craig, John. "Brothers sentenced in UI murder." *Spokesman Review*, 19 Nov 2005. www.spokesman.com/stories/2005/nov/19/brothers-sentenced-in-ui-murder. Accessed 8 Oct 22.

Dubner, Stephen J. "These Jobs Were Not Posted on ZipRecruiter." *Freakonomics Radio*, 25 Aug 2021. freakonomics.com/podcast/these-jobs-were-not-posted-on-ziprecruiter. Accessed 8 Oct 2022.

Ganzer, Tony. "What we need is trust." *AnthonyGanzer.com*, 17 April 2019. www.anthonyganzer.com/public-speaking/what-we-need-is-trust. Accessed 5 Nov 2022.

Google News Initiative. *Google*. newsinitiative.withgoogle.com. Accessed 8 Oct 2022.

Gross, Jenny. "How Finland Is Teaching a Generation to Spot Misinformation." *The New York Times*, 10 Jan 2023. https://www.nytimes.com/2023/01/10/world/europe/finland-misinformation-classes.html. Accessed 26 Jan 2023.

Haugh, Katy and Jem Collins. "'I Was Shocked How Big The Drinking Culture Was': Journalism's Difficult Relationship With Alcohol." *Journo Resources*, 2 Jan 2020. www.journoresources.org.uk/journalists-alcohol-problem-relationship. Accessed 8 Oct 2022.

Henley, Jon. "How Finland starts its fight against fake news in primary schools." *The Guardian*, 29 Jan 2020. www.the-guardian.com/world/2020/jan/28/fact-from-fiction-fin-lands-new-lessons-in-combating-fake-news. Accessed 26 Jan 2023.

Jones, Jeffrey M. "Confidence in U.S. Institutions Down; Average at New Low." *Gallup*, 5 July 2022. news.gallup.com/poll/394283/confidence-institutions-down-average-new-low.aspx. Accessed 8 Oct 2022.

Joseph, Ted. "A Study of Alcohol Use by Reporters and Editors." *Newspaper Research Journal*, vol. 4, no. 2, January 1983, pp. 3-8.

Lippmann, Walter. *Public Opinion*. Harcourt, Brace and Company, 1922.

Lorenz, Taylor. "Personal branding is more powerful than ever." *NiemanLab*, December 2018. www.niemanlab.org/2018/12/personal-branding-is-more-powerful-than-ever. Accessed 8 Oct 2022.

Martin, Fiona and Tim Dwyer. "Churnalism on the rise as news sites fill up with shared content and wire copy." *The Conversation*, 12 June 2012. theconversation.com/churnalism-on-the-rise-as-news-sites-fill-up-with-shared-content-and-wire-copy-7859. Accessed 14 Oct 2022.

Murrow, Edward R. RTDNA Convention, 15 October 1958. rtdna.org/content/edward_r_murrow_s_1958_wires_lights_in_a_box_speech. Accessed 13 April 2019.

Reinardy, Scott and Lawrie Zion. "Cutting Deeper: U.S. Newspapers Wipeout Jobs and Alter Career Identities." *Journalism Practice*, 2019. kuscholarworks.ku.edu/bitstream/handle/1808/29947/cutting%20deeper.pdf;jsessionid=50F44D1C368A7F128AA6CD53061DB6B9?sequence=1 . Accessed 8 Oct 2022.

Schafer, Jack. "The Whiskey Rebellion." *Slate*, 2 Jan 2008. slate.com/news-and-politics/2008/01/why-booze-and-cigarettes-are-essential-for-good-journalism.html. Accessed 8 Oct 2022.

Summers, Leila. "Crash leaves 1 dead, 1 critical; UI fraternity members thrown from motorcycle." *Moscow-Pullman Daily News*, 20 Sept 2004. dnews.com/local/crash-leaves-1-dead-1-critical-ui-fraternity-members-thrown-from-motorcycle/article_6ee650e4-1390-5466-beb1-35a9fd7be031.html. Accessed 8 Oct 2022.

Swart, Tara. "Study into the mental resilience of journalists." *TaraSwart.com*, May 2017. www.taraswart.com/mental-resilience-of-journalists. Accessed 8 Oct 2022.

"Trust in America: Do Americans trust the news media?" *Pew Research Center*, 5 Jan 2022. www.pewresearch.org/2022/01/05/trust-in-america-do-americans-trust-the-news-media. Accessed 8 Oct 2022.

Walker, Mason. "U.S. newsroom employment has fallen 26% since 2008." *Pew Research Center*, 13 July 2021. www.pewresearch.org/fact-tank/2021/07/13/u-s-newsroom-employment-has-fallen-26-since-2008. Accessed 8 Oct 2022.

7. Leaving daily news

Godin, Seth. *Linchpin: Are You Indispensable? How to drive your career and create a remarkable future.* Little, Brown Book Group, 2010

Lewis, C.S. A *Grief Observed*. HarperCollins, 1961.

Mehta, Aaron. "Colbert's super PAC raises serious money from 'donors' with silly names." *The Center for Public Integrity*, 31 Jan 2012. publicintegrity.org/politics/colberts-super-pac-raises-serious-money-from-donors-with-silly-names. Accessed 28 Oct 2022.

Oddisee. "Oddisee "You Know Who You Are" ft. Olivier Daysoul (Acoustic Version)." *YouTube*, uploaded by Oddisee, 12 June 2012. www.youtube.com/watch?v=RgopVOg2ifk.

Prokop, Andrew. "How Stephen Colbert taught Americans about Super PACs." *Vox*, 15 May 2015. https://www.vox.com/2014/6/4/5776676/stephen-colbert-super-pac-study. Accessed 28 Oct 2022.

Yeager, Melissa. "It's been 4 years since Stephen Colbert created a super PAC — where did all that money go?" *Sunlight Foun-*

dation, 30 Sept 2015. sunlightfoundation.com/2015/09/30/its-been-four-years-since-stephen-colbert-created-a-super-pac-where-did-all-that-money-go. Accessed 28 Oct 2022.

About the Author

Tony Ganzer has spent decades as an award-winning journalist, podcaster, and international communications professional in the U.S. and Europe. He is a former correspondent for the Swiss Broadcasting Corporation, and also worked as a public radio host and reporter for major market outlets in Germany and the U.S., reporting on Nobel laureates, asylum seekers, heads of state, and many others. His journalism work was published by, among others, National Public Radio, the BBC, Deutsche Welle, and PRI. He holds an M.A. in International Relations and World Order from the University of Leicester, and an M.B.A. from Youngstown State University. He earned his B.S. in Journalism from the University of Idaho. He was awarded the Robert Bosch Foundation Fellowship for young American leaders for a year professional placement in Germany. He is also recipient of the Arthur F. Burns Fellowship for American journalists to work with German media outlets, and was named a next generation leader by the German Marshall Fund. He likes bread baking for family and friends, playing guitar, and exploring faith stories through his Faith Full Podcast. He speaks fluent German, and a bit of French on a good day.

Learn more at www.anthonyganzer.com

Printed in Great Britain
by Amazon

38228924R00094